2009 Poetry Competition for 11

I have a
dream 2009
Words to change the world

Martin Luther King

John Lennon

# Poems From The UK

Edited by Helen Davies

First published in Great Britain in 2009 by:

 Young**Writers**

Young Writers
Remus House
Coltsfoot Drive
Peterborough
PE2 9JX
Telephone: 01733 890066
Website: www.youngwriters.co.uk

All Rights Reserved
Book Design by Spencer Hart & Tim Christian
© Copyright Contributors 2009
SB ISBN 978-1-84924 389 6

# Foreword

'I Have a Dream 2009' is a series of poetry collections written by 11 to 18-year-olds from schools and colleges across the UK and overseas. Pupils were invited to send us their poems using the theme 'I Have a Dream'. Selected entries range from dreams they've experienced to childhood fantasies of stardom and wealth, through inspirational poems of their dreams for a better future and of people who have influenced and inspired their lives.

The series is a snapshot of who and what inspires, influences and enthuses young adults of today. It shows an insight into their hopes, dreams and aspirations of the future and displays how their dreams are an escape from the pressures of today's modern life. Young Writers are proud to present this anthology, which is truly inspired and sure to be an inspiration to all who read it.

# Contents

# The Poems

# Alone

Sound of footsteps all around,
The hustle and bustle of the crowd,
A teardrop drops onto the ground,
But no one glances or looks around,
Scared. Lonely. Forgotten.

She sits on the street,
With no one but herself,
Money might not be everything,
But she could do with some wealth.
Scared. Lonely. Forgotten.

She hears nothing,
But the sound of her heartbeat,
Telling her she lives to see another day,
She feels nothing,
But the disapproving glares from passers-by
As they avoid her feet,
Scared. Lonely. Forgotten.

A shiver runs down her spine,
As she remembers the night she left everything behind,
She remembers running,
Running from her troubles.
Scared. Lonely. Forgotten.

Her eyes fill up with water,
As she dreams of her life before,
She was her daughter,
How did she become embedded in that war?
Scared. Lonely. Forgotten.

Is being on the streets better than being at home?
Every day's a battle,
With no place to call your own,
You've no one to trust, you're completely alone.
Scared. Lonely. Forgotten.

**Kosi Atkinson (13)**
Bushfield Community College, Peterborough

# Living And Learning

Today I don't have any words,
I don't have any inspiration,
I've been looking at my pen with frustration,
I don't think you'll comprehend,
But at least, try to apprehend.

I've just been thinking about life,
About what we are trying to strive,
What we aim for,
And what we've done before.

I've finally reached a conclusion:
That I cannot dive into illusions,
Thinking that life is perfect,
Instead, I have to reflect . . .
Then correct.

Reflect in the way I see others,
Correct it,
And consider them as brothers,
Reflect in the way I see myself,
Correct it,
And leave my old self on a shelf.

I wasted too much time trying to understand life,
In fear that someone would strike me with a knife,
The hardest thing for me to learn,
Was that we live and we learn.

I learned to smile at people who hate me,
To show them that maybe there was no reason to hate,
I learnt to say goodbye to what I loved,
To stop more hearts from being shoved,
I learned that nobody is strong enough,
Even though they pretend to be tough,
I learned to laugh and to show what I feel
To live every moment feeling real,
I learned to have fun,
Taking responsibility for what I'd done,
I learned to use my heart,
But at the same time as being smart,

I learned to listen and pay attention
Forgetting that my world had only one dimension
I learnt to be strong and fight,
Hoping that my future would be bright.

I've been looking at the time with determination,
Seeing people without discrimination,
Observing nature with admiration,
Confronting my fears without hesitation.

I've realised that life is too short to be wasted,
And at one point, I'm going to be devastated,
At one point, life is going to throw stones at me,
But that won't stop me from trying to be free,
At one point, walls will be built in my way,
But that won't make my virtue stray.

I've realised that happiness makes us soft,
Problems make us strong,
Sadness makes me human,
And hope is what keeps us going.

**Delba Cristina De Oliveira (14)**
Bushfield Community College, Peterborough

# Pure Happiness

Pure happiness does not come from little pills,
Or even from life's cheap new thrills,
You cannot buy it, sell it or take it,
You cannot fight it or even fake it.
For when it's there you shall smile,
And all the work will seem worthwhile,
So if this your true desire,
Then quickly reignite your fire,
Strive for what you want in life,
Be it a job, be it a wife,
One person can make this happiness true,
Believe me now that person is you!

**Samantha Ladds (14)**
Bushfield Community College, Peterborough

# Mother's Poem

A mother cradled her wailing daughter,
Pouring her unquenchable love over her,
Like soft, warm water,
But still she continued to bawl.
The baby kicked with her chubby legs,
Trying to break free from her mother's tight grasp,
Wanting instead to walk.

The mother was too caught up in fond memories,
Of when her child was helpless
And completely dependent on her.
But she couldn't ignore her cries,
For her first taste of freedom and independence.
Eventually, she put her down to let her enter
A new exciting world of discovery.

And sure enough, the day came when the mother witnessed
Her daughter's first kiss under the old apple tree,
Where she herself had experienced that special moment,
Those many summers ago.
She once again dwelled upon the past,
To when her daughter was just taking those first steps
Into the unknown.
Soon, adolescence would dawn upon her little girl
And the house would be filled with sobs from a broken heart,
Shouts of, 'But that's not fair!' and,
'Mum I need new curlers for my hair.'

Years came, and years went by
And the mother wiped a tear from her eye,
As she saw her daughter walk down the aisle.
How had time gone by so fast?
How was it that her confused teenager
Was to be married
To the love of her life?

A few years went by,
And a mother cradled her wailing daughter,
Pouring her unquenchable love over her,
Like soft, warm water,
But still she continued to bawl.

The baby kicked with her chubby legs,
Trying to break free of her mother's tight grasp,
Wanting instead to walk . . .
So you wonder,
What's the point of this poem?
What's the message I want people to receive?
Well it's this:
Never, never, never dwell on the past,
But instead,
Always, always, always embrace the future,
And enjoy the treasures that life brings!

**Jenny Allum (13)**
Bushfield Community College, Peterborough

# I Am Your Dream

When the only way to reach your dream
Is to climb, I will accompany you,
When obstacles get in your way, I will help you,
When everything seems to fail,
I will encourage you,
It does not take a genius to do something,
But takes hard work and dedication to master it,
I am your dream.

**Cherry Williams (13)**
Bushfield Community College, Peterborough

# You Can Do It!

When was the last time you heard these words:
*You can do it!*
Do you have to delve into your mind to find it?
Or can you not remember?

Everybody needs motivation to keep going,
Without it, we shrivel into nothing, given up without thought,
Cowering away. Hiding. Not to carry on,
Thinking there's no one to turn to.

What about your mum, dad, sister, aunt?
Or are they too far to reach? Do you feel ostracised?
Well you're not! They are there!
*Hear those words: You can do it!*

Suddenly, you no longer cower under your bed,
You emerge like a butterfly, out of a cocoon,
That lonely existence, as you burst out,
Free! Strong! Ready for anything!

Whatever your goal you strive for,
Whatever the obstacle you clear it,
For success is not easily achieved,
But with a helping hand; it's success that you believe.

**Jamie Plumb (14)**
Bushfield Community College, Peterborough

# Never, Never, Never Give Up

Even when life is not what it seems,
It will all work out,
Have faith - no doubt,
Never, never, never give up.

We all have rights to dream,
You have to be driven to achieve success,
So sort it all out - fix this mess,
Never, never, never give up.

So who do you want to be?
It is time you let it show,
'cause your change will be gone - before you know,
Never, never, never give up.

Don't be happy with blending in,
You are the light in the dark,
Don't dim out - be that spark,
Never, never, never give up.

You only get one chance to live,
So live your life as you want it to be,
All you need to do is believe - you'll see,
Never, never, never give up.

**Jessica Munday (13)**
Bushfield Community College, Peterborough

# Together And One

Change is the most complicated word in the world,
We can change the world and have men reunited
                              and nations in peace,
As one voice, not as separate nations we can change,
In Afghanistan bodies and rubble litter the streets,
Missiles lighten the midnight sky and echo the day,
Not as one nation, together we can end war and terrorism.

**Daniel Pascoe (13)**
Dene Community School of Technology, Peterlee

# My Inspirations!

The world I live in is poor and selfish,
We may have what we want,
But others have nothing,
Men die heroes fighting in wars,
There is poverty in Africa,
But we are all fine here,
Our lives may not be perfect,
We should think of others for a change.

I hope that one day this happens.

I get cared for, I get food,
Why can't everybody's life be perfect?
Why can't the fighting go away?
Most of us know what we want and get it,
This is my dream,
I am lucky, I am alive,
Why can't we all forget our differences?

I hope that one day this happens.

All diseases should have a cure,
The world is a good place, in most countries,
Were we all made for great lives?
Or just great lives for the rich and famous?
Everybody is different,
Hungry, poor, young, old people without clean water,
But why in Africa?
We should all be equally healthy and fit.

I hope one day this happens!

**Lucy Brooksbank (11)**
Dene Community School of Technology, Peterlee

# I Want This To Change!

Animals becoming extinct because they are being
Hunted for their fur and meat.

I want this to change!

Some people don't have enough food to eat because
Their parents don't seem to care or are poor.

I want this to change!

People dying all over the world because of
Diseases that can be easily treated.

I want this to change!

All the countries that are richer than others,
And want to be richer.

I want this to change!

Declaring war over stupid things like oil and
Equipment like in Iraq.

I want this to change!

Robbing banks, shoplifting and mugging,
All for their own good.

I want this to change!

Murders, rape and abuse to innocent people,
Left to die in their blood.

I want this to change!

And this is my dream!

**Liam Bell (13)**
Dene Community School of Technology, Peterlee

# What I Want To Change!

I have a dream,
This world should change,
All fighting, wars and arguments,
Oils and equipment can just be shared,
This place would be far better.

I have a dream,
This world should change,
All evilness to animals,
Hunting them for their meat and fur,
They may all become extinct.

I have a dream,
This world should change,
The drugs and alcohol,
It may cause criminals,
This makes people scared.

I have a dream,
This world should change,
All people should help,
People die of diseases,
That are easily treated.

I have a dream,
This world should change,
Pollution to the environment,
All people can help,
Just stop littering.

**Shannon Southward (14)**
Dene Community School of Technology, Peterlee

# Overcrowded Prisons

*Bang!*
The gavel is hit,
*Clonk!*
The cell door is locked.

We share a cell,
The five of us,
We share a sink,
The five of us.

There will be petty thieves,
And serial killers,
Locked up together,
In prison forever.

We share a cell,
The five of us,
We share a sink,
The five of us.

*Smack!*
Inmate down,
*Smack!*
Prison officer down.

We share a cell,
The five of us,
We share a sink,
The five of us.

**Michael House (14)**
Dene Community School of Technology, Peterlee

# My Awesome Poem

If everyone was equal, we could all have an opinion,
All have food,
And we would all be able to communicate in the same language.

If people didn't hate each other, there would be no wars
And people of every colour and race could be friends.

If we started to help people we could have good relationships
And what if people weren't judged by the way they looked
But the way they acted?

If there wasn't a difference between rich and poor,
We could all have a good life.

If every child had a free education,
They would have a better chance of getting a career.

If teens didn't take drugs, mug people and kill people
For no reason,
How many people would still be alive today?

If we donated money to charities,
The less fortunate people in the world could have the
Basic essentials in life,
And they could be vaccinated to stop disease
Spreading and killing people.

If everyone was the same and there was no hate
And hate and aggression,
Think how different the world would be today.

**Liam Price (13)**
Dene Community School of Technology, Peterlee

# My Mum

She cooks,
She cleans,
She cares.

But she still has time for me.

She works a full time job.

But she still has time for me.

She often tells me how she loves me so.

She's kind,
She's funny,
She's caring.

She's like a best friend,
Yet easier to talk to.

When I'm poorly, she worries,
When she's poorly, I worry.

I love my mam,
And she loves me.

She always wants the best for me,
She thinks of me before herself,
She understands my worries and fears.

I'm so lucky to have a mum like this.

**Zoe Taylor (12)**
Dene Community School of Technology, Peterlee

13

# My Poem

She cooks and cleans,
And washes my jeans.

She goes to the shops to buy me clothes,
She always looks beautiful and it shows.

She drives me up to the gymnastics,
To let me do my cartwheels and back-flips.

She loves her holidays in the sun,
Because it's the place to have fun.

She likes to make cakes for special occasions,
But most of the time, it's just for relations.

She likes to talk all the time,
And I am sitting making this poem rhyme.

She always sings in the bath,
And hears my dad coming up the path.

She likes to hear the birds in the tree,
And says, 'Listen, they're singing to me!'

My mam is the best,
And wears her heart on her chest.

She is slim like my dad,
She is never really sad.

**Ashleigh Dunleavy (11)**
Dene Community School of Technology, Peterlee


# I Have A Dream

I have a dream that one day the whole world will bring peace,
Stop the violence and join hands,
Stop the hatred and make friends,
Stop the arguing and make love,
Stop the wars and make peace,
I have a dream today.

**Paige Ann Robertson (13)**
Dene Community School of Technology, Peterlee

# I Have A Dream

Things in my life aren't up to scratch,
Oh no Sunderland lost another match,
In my hometown there's nothing flash,
It's covered all over in trash.

Come on people change our ways!

We should be living the life of luxury,
Not committing adultery,
We shouldn't be mean,
Try and keep our lives clean.

Come on people change our ways!

Sitting in the house all cosy and warm,
Not thinking of all the harm.

Come on people change our ways!

Why call people names, for who they are?
This is what started the war,
People are black, people are white,
So yeah, get over it, right?
People are who they are,
Not for the make of their car,
Come on people, stop being harsh,
Come on people, change our ways!

**Sophie Ord (13)**
Dene Community School of Technology, Peterlee

# Treat The World With Respect

I have a dream . . .

The world will one day be a better place,
If only we care for what we've got.

Have you noticed it's getting hot?
That's global warming taking effect,
This poor world is suffering from hate and neglect.

Open your eyes and look around, everything is not sound,
Take a look at Iraq, look at how they are suffering from attacks.

All the dirty children scurry to their feet,
To escape the devastation the bombs do seek,
As they beg alone on the scruffy streets,
Everything they once had, has now ended in misery,
Do people not realise they only wanted to play?

Treat the world with respect and not neglect;
This is the message from my poem.

Treat the world with respect because
You don't know what you've got until it's gone.

So take this opportunity to say,
'I will treat this world with respect and not neglect today.'

This is my dream!

**Sarah Jane Broughton (14)**
Dene Community School of Technology, Peterlee

# Completing My Wish

I have a dream to,
Let the world rest in peace,
And let people be happy,
Why do we have food and water,
And over Africa they don't have any?

Think about this for just a minute,
And maybe you can join my dream too,
Think about others and not yourself,
Saving lives and caring for people's health!

My dream may come true, as long as you believe,
People caring for one another,
All it takes is for you to believe,
You may have lost a close friend or a brother!

Soldiers fight and represent our country,
Battling on the frontline,
Risking their own lives, they've done that plenty,
This world has too many crimes!

Why don't you believe in what I wish?
Why can't everyone be equal?
You may think you live in a world of peace,
But really we're different people!

**Bethany Rippon (13)**
Dene Community School of Technology, Peterlee

# I Have A Dream

I have a dream that the things I want to change
Are people who have bad lives,
Everyone should be the same so they don't get picked on,
People who have bad lives should go in groups of fives,
And work their way to the top and their bad lives will be gone.

Everyone with good lives will be fit and healthy,
Because they have over three meals a day,
Everyone fit and healthy will be strong and wealthy,
And everything will be OK.

People who have a normal life,
Will have been looked after by their mum and dad,
Because they are husband and wife,
You will never get treated bad.

Because you are wealthy and you're fit and healthy,
You will have a good job, house and car,
If you are not fit and healthy and not even wealthy,
You will not be able to go to the bar.

If you are poor, then you can't go on a tour,
You can't go on holiday when you want to,
If you are really poor and you go in the sewer,
Then you can't do anything that you want to do.

**Talia Muncaster (14)**
Dene Community School of Technology, Peterlee

# I Have A Dream

I want the world to change,
I want the bad to stop,
People causing global warming,
People taking illegal drugs,
I think this has gone too far,
And I can't take it anymore.

Brave soldiers in the war,
Risking their lives all the more,
I don't think this is fair,
And I think this should stop.

Poor animals being shot,
More and more, all the time,
I want this to stop,
To make the world better.

African people with no food,
Putting them in a mood,
All those people with no home,
Looking for shelter, the streets they roam.

Crime should be stopped,
Guns should be banned,
And the world would be a better place.

**Jodie Lowery (13)**
Dene Community School of Technology, Peterlee

# Breaking The Boundaries

One day we'll break the boundaries,
And change the world forever,
Science is a big part of it,
But we need to work forever.

Things will be available,
That we've never seen before,
We'll solve all these problems,
Like war and global warming.

But the scars they'll leave,
Will be with us forever,
One day we'll change the world,
And heal the scars and curse.

But we need education,
And inspiration is all around us,
To change a life, can change the world,
Like MLK or Winston Churchill.

We need to work together,
And as MLK said,
'I have a dream,'
This is my dream.

**James Hyde (13)**
Dene Community School of Technology, Peterlee

# I Have A Dream

In this world there are things I want to change,
Everything back to normal again,
Everyone equal, everyone share,
People with cancer need better care,
People with drink problems have no excuse,
To give their kids and family so much abuse,
On the news and in the papers,
It's all about people doing crimes,
Knives and guns or just their hands,
Lots of people getting killed,
Over silly things like the colour of their skin,
Teens getting drunk or high on drugs,
Even the nicest ones turn into thugs,
Friends fall out and have fights,
They get arrested and put in jail overnight,
If the person they fought with
Dies during the night,
They get sent to prison, maybe for life,
You may think these things are strange,
But these are the things that I want to change.

**Adam Birt (13)**
Dene Community School of Technology, Peterlee


# Differences

What is the difference between black and white?
They are just the same as us.

What is the difference between fat and skinny?

What is the difference between rich and poor?

What is the difference between bombs and guns?

What is the difference between kids and men?

*There is no difference in death.*

**Liam Scott (11)**
Dene Community School of Technology, Peterlee

# My Poem: I Have A Dream

The things that differ in the world,
Are races and cultures,
That have lived and died,
We could make it better if we tried.

Vandals, mobs and criminal acts,
Have worthless means that good people lack,
Mams and dads and all the rest,
Always try to teach you the best.

Leaders always end up in wars,
They never see what's in store,
Money, resources and all the oil,
Couldn't solve this turmoil.

The people who taught me this and more,
Are my parents and what they saw,
The people I value they all said this,
And they are the ones I'm going to miss.

I know I won't get involved in drugs,
Junkies, criminals and mindless thugs.

**Michael Gray (13)**
Dene Community School of Technology, Peterlee


# My Perfect World

My perfect world won't be destroyed,
No pollution,
A world where everyone's the same,
Where everyone is together,
No one will go hungry,
Where violence is a thing of the past,
Everyone in the world will have a good education,
No one is different,
Please help the people who need our help,
Everyone deserves a chance to live to the best of their abilities.

**Michelle Foster (15)**
Dene Community School of Technology, Peterlee

# Believe

Try and hold on,
Don't give up,
Life's too short to give up on trying,
So, don't stop believing,
You know you can succeed,
Keep on believing,
Keep on achieving,
Keep on crying,
Head up high,
Reach the sky,
And things won't seem as bad,
Keep on believing,
Keep on achieving,
Keep on trying,
You can do it.

Everything can change,
Things will be different,
So believe, believe,
Believe.

**Chelsea Jeffrey (13)**
Dene Community School of Technology, Peterlee

# Endangered Animals

E very day a polar bear passes away
N otice how the penguins fade
D ying out, the bears quickly disappear
A nother animal dies every day
N ever-ending line of species dying out,
G azing out, the wildlife is slowly fading
E xtremely quickly animals go extinct
R ed squirrels dying poisoned by the grey
E ndangered animals are dying quickly
D o something to help to save wildlife.

**Elisha Daniels (13)**
Dene Community School of Technology, Peterlee

# Our Life

Life is precious,
Life is loving, or was . . .

Life is short,
And getting shorter each day,
We can change this,
We can all change this.

Animals are becoming extinct,
Plants are dying,
Soon it could be us.

The world is giving us chances to change it,
But we are just walking straight past them.

Soon those chances will run out,
They'll run out without us knowing,
The world will be dead,
The animals will be dead,
Everything will be dead.

Now's the time to change our life . . .

**Rebecca Tupling (12)**
Dene Community School of Technology, Peterlee

# War

There is a war going on,
Many innocent people are being murdered,
We could stop this,
If only we sat down and talked,
Many soldiers have been sent out,
But it is not making a difference,
If only we sat down and talked,
This war will keep going on,
We need to sit down and talk.

**Corey Calvert (12)**
Dene Community School of Technology, Peterlee

# My World!

When I entered this world it was full of love,
I thought to myself, *it was sent from above,*
No killing, no fighting, no time for more wars,
It's such a shame, it's not like that anymore.

I wish it would end, it's driving me round the bend.

There's people out there with no food or drink,
Now that's the time to stop and think,
We take it for granted, our education,
We need to help others, no time for hesitation.

Wish it would end, it's driving me round the bend.

Dame Kelly Holmes is one of a kind,
She has helped the poor, the sick and the blind,
She used her talents to help the others,
Even the children without any mothers.

I wish it would end, it's driving me round the *bend!*

**Shelby Marie Jones (14)**
Dene Community School of Technology, Peterlee

# Change?

Can we change our ways?

The way we take advantage of what we've got.

The way we treat different people.

The way we fight without a care!

You may think violence is right,
And in some ways you are right,
But if we fight without a care,
Will there be anything left?

So . . .

Can we change our ways?

**Charlotte Legg (13)**
Dene Community School of Technology, Peterlee

25

# Litter

Dropping litter is a criminal offence - fact,
Litter bins are there for a reason,
More streets are becoming less intact,
Litter is dropped in every season.

This is now the time to put a full stop,
To all the litter taking the drop,
This is now damaging your city, town.
Litter dropping needs to be cut down,
This is now getting a disgrace,
Bins are there in every place.

Where would you rather live?
A tidy clean place or
A dirty scruffy disgrace?

Answer that question in your head,
Because littering needs to be put to bed!

**Daniel Turner (13)**
Dene Community School of Technology, Peterlee


# Do We Even Care?

Do we even care,
About the animals out there?
Do you even care,
About the world out there?

The animals are dying because of our stupid ways,
The world is now dying because of our stupid ways.

Do we even care,
About the animals out there?
Do we even care,
About the world out there?

Large amounts of litter cramping our tiny streets,
Catching and killing the animals we have left.

**Neive Mallory (13)**
Dene Community School of Technology, Peterlee


26

# Pollution

I have a dream,
I have a small dream today,
But it's a big one tomorrow,
People complain about wars,
Wars around the world,
But there's a bigger war,
Just under our noses,
A war between us and Earth,
Pollution,
Pollution is our worst enemy,
The thing we create,
So actively,
It might not effect us now,
But it's the future,
The future will feel it,
Save our world.

**Jordan Birt (13)**
Dene Community School of Technology, Peterlee

# Freedom

The sound of freedom reminds me of peace,
For freedom reminds me of cheeping birds,
Like bears getting released into the wild,
Like on an open field with flocks of sheep,
It is up to us now to change the world,
To be free of all the wars going on,
Like lots of people working together,
Until the working day is completed,
Freedom should last forever and ever,
If only our troubles were defeated,
In the future there could be changes made,
To be free, safe and have our planet saved.

**Jennifer Hutton (12)**
Dene Community School of Technology, Peterlee

# Let Us Not Hide

Let us not hide in the shadows,
We can help,
Help the world from destruction,
Everyone can help,
Everyone has a choice,
Let us change the world,
Stop pollution,
Let us change the world,
Stop poaching,
Let us save the animals,
Not kill them,
Let us make global warming,
No more,
Let us stop the fighting,
And live in world peace!

**Ryan Coates (13)**
Dene Community School of Technology, Peterlee

# Inspiration

I have a dream!

Greenhouse gases, pollution, global warming,
Forests being cut down, animals dying,
Soon to be extinct.

My dream is for all this to stop!

Rivers running dry, children dying from starvation,
People drinking dirty water,
People dying in wars.

My dream is for all this to stop!

Poachers killing animals for their flesh and fur,
Sharks and dolphins dying because they get caught in fishing nets.

My dream is for all this to stop!

**Rachel Pounder (12)**
Dene Community School of Technology, Peterlee

# Keep The World Safe

Love
Hate
Pressure and
Glory
Is what the world is covered in
Love
Hate
Pressure and
Glory
Is what we're living in,
If we keep this world safe,
We may live forever,
We can stop the violence,
If we work together.

**Chloe Cordner (12)**
Dene Community School of Technology, Peterlee

# Street Corners

For once I would love to turn a corner,
Without being hassled by devious youths,
For once I would love to walk on the ground,
Rather than glass, plastic and chewing gum,
For once I would love a good storyline,
Rather than murder, theft and alcohol,
Together we can help clean the corners,
Together we must unite to save us,
To save everyone, the sun and the Earth,
Now is the time to do something to help,
Rather than letting the world's killers win,
For now it is possible to do it,
We can, we shall and we will defeat them,
We can, we shall and we will defeat them.

**Emma Wood (13)**
Dene Community School of Technology, Peterlee

# My World

People in our world,
Are keeping us safe,
Risking their lives,
So we can keep ours.

How? How? How
Can we save the world?
Why? Why? Why
Is the world dying on us?

Soldiers, doctors fight to save us,
Global warming needs us to help,
Recycle a couple of tins,
Don't forget, put them in bins,
By doing that it would save the planet.

**Rachel Broadhead (13)**
Dene Community School of Technology, Peterlee

# Modern War

*Bang! Bang! Bang!*
One by one,
They fall,
In the face of disaster,
We're looking strong.

In this wasted country,
They plan in tunnels,
We go in deserted towns,
Ghost towns.

We travel far and wide,
Meet new faces everywhere,
Come into the danger zone -
Scared for life.

**Thomas Burdess (14)**
Dene Community School of Technology, Peterlee

# We Have A Life

We have a life,
We have a life to enjoy,
Not to play war,
We have a life to love,
And not to kill,
Life is happiness,
Not sadness,
Friends for friends is what we like,
Enemies for enemies is what we hate,
Life is not meant for sadness,
But for happiness and joy,
'Together we are the future!'

**Emma Yuill (12)**
Dene Community School of Technology, Peterlee

# The World Will Never Be The Same

Time is running out,
People dropping one by one,
Animal extinction dropping down,
The world will never be the same.

Saving the planet?
It's up to you,
Recycle, don't litter,
The world will never be the same.

It is like a clock ticking,
One, two, down for the count,
The world will never be the same.

**Jordan Hodgson (14)**
Dene Community School of Technology, Peterlee

# Animal Issues

You know that bag you carry?
You know that coat you wear?
You know those boots you walk on?
Do you even care,
About where they came from?
Together we can stop this,
Animals both timid and wild,
Together we can stop this,
Animals killed for your pride,
Together we can stop this,
We can, we shall, we must.

**Charlotte Churchill (12)**
Dene Community School of Technology, Peterlee

# World Destruction

*Bang! Bang!*
Here comes a bullet,
My friend, shot two times,
Afghanistan soldiers,
Killing everyone.

British soldiers being killed,
American soldiers being killed,
Death is all around.

Weeping mothers want to die,
Why?

**Connor Neal (12)**
Dene Community School of Technology, Peterlee

# I Have A Dream

One guy wanted society,
To be a better place,
Stopping racism and violence,
No need for guns, knives and mace.

With remarkable footsteps to follow in,
Can *we*, can I, change the world,
Preventing awful things happening,
All the things we've heard?

One man had a dream,
And got way to the top,
He started with a record company,
And he didn't stop.

Knowing that it's possible,
Can *we*, can I, change the world?
Putting barriers behind us,
Letting our minds fly wild like a newly freed bird?

One woman was just a helper,
Thought of only others,
Making people's hurt lives better,
She never thought she was above us.

Knowing our luck,
Can *we,* can I, change the world?
Helping those much less fortunate,
Whose lives seem absurd?

Will I make a difference?
Can I fully achieve?
Doing something hugely fulfilling,
And have my old opinions leave?

I think I want to make a difference,
As crazy as it may seem,
I'm going to do *something* special . . .

*I, have a dream!*

**Thomas Ricketts (13)**
Harris School, Rugby

33

# I Have A Dream

We all dream about different things,
Of course that's what's true,
But have you ever thought to ask,
What someone else dreams about too?

Do we dream about the future,
Or dream about the past?
Do we think about that latest game?
Giving those baddies a good old blast!

Do we dream about romance?
Our latest lover to be,
Or do we dream about success?
Our faces covered with glee.

Do we dream about our work
And what jobs we have to do?
Do we dream about the new fashion,
Those beautiful brand new shoes?

Do we dream about our money,
Saving it up in towers?
Or are we envious of others' money,
Wishing that it was ours?

Do we dream about our friends
And all the joy to be had?
Or do we dream about our enemies,
Slowly going mad?

What we have learnt today has no need to be discovered,
I really think that no one here is at all bothered!

**Luke Sapiano (12)**
Harris School, Rugby

# I Have A Dream

I have a dream,
Which sails away,
In the sails of a boat,
And on the wings of a bird,
Flying high into the sky.

The dream soars down,
And turns into reality,
I *can* achieve it, I know I can,
The dream is there - that's all I need.

The dream launches me forward,
Gives me a push in life,
Influences me, thrives in me,
Enables me to live life and live it to the full.

In a few years time,
With a bit of training,
I'll be famous,
Doing what I love the most.

All I need,
To be a champion sailor,
All I will ever need,
To go far in life,
Is the dream.

**Bethanie Pelloquin (12)**
Harris School, Rugby


# Peace

P eace on Earth is what we want,
E verybody deserves a chance in life,
A nger never solved a lot,
C are and love is what our kids want,
E njoy the life you have today.

**Jack Finch (12)**
Harris School, Rugby

# Lifelong Dream

He had a dream,
He fought for his right,
He knew he could,
He knew he would,
He never gave up,
He never stopped believing,
Long walk to freedom,
He had a dream,
He met his dream.

He saw the world,
Where black and white,
Lived side by side,
Respect and hatred,
He had a dream,
To make that stop,
To make equal,
Equal,
Not black and white,
One big family,
Long walk to freedom,
He had a dream,
He met his dream.

**Matthew Gorman (12)**
Harris School, Rugby

# I Have A Dream

I have a dream that every animal in the world is free and kind,
They will be able to roam around wherever they like,
Nobody will mistreat them or hurt them in any way,
And a world full of peace,
And all of the wars in Afghanistan will be stopped,
No burglaries or murders,
Or any form of abuse in our world.

**Ben Suckling (13)**
Harris School, Rugby

# All About Money

I dream about money,
Some may call this sad,
But money to me, is like a bee with honey,
And money makes me glad.

I don't care about friends,
Some may call this mean,
But friends aren't worth their weight in gold,
And money makes girls keen.

Mum and Dad can go to hell,
You could call this extreme,
But Larkin was right in 'This be the Verse',
And what have they done for me?

Christmas dinner was flat,
My birthday too,
All of them sad and quiet, alone I sat,
And no, 'Happy birthday to you'.

I dream about friends,
And family would be great,
Cos family are there through bad and good,
And everyone needs a mate.

**James Howe (12)**
Harris School, Rugby

# I Have A Dream

I have a dream,
That mums and dads love and care for their children.

That families don't fight anymore.

Wars are over.

People lived in peace and harmony.

**Leanne Adams (13)**
Harris School, Rugby

# My Dream

I once had a dream,
that my family would be allowed to grow up living equally with
Peace, love and faith.

Without being judged by rank or name
or by race or even who we would follow.
Allowing love to destroy and banish
Hatred, racism, greed, injustice!

Brother with brother, hand in hand,
Standing together not fighting each other, only
Loving and respecting each other.

I still dream . . .
That cruelty, hate, judgement and crime
will be abolished and leave the Earth forever.
Always and never ever return!

That is when all is worth living,
This will be my dream, forever.

**James Was (13)**
Harris School, Rugby

# I Have A Dream!

I hope for people to have a home,
I hope for people to live for long.

I hope for you to come back to me,
I hope for you to see what I see.

I look at you, your stars so bright,
I look at you, all day and night!

I see you in a stormy night,
I see you in the sun so bright.

I need you now more than ever I say!
I need you now more than ever I pray!

**Emily Thomas (13)**
Harris School, Rugby

# The World Can Change!

The world's been changed by many people,
Good and bad,
Sometimes it's for the better or for the worse,
That's sad,
But at the moment there seems there is no bad
Because it looks like people are quite glad.

Some people in the world,
Like Mother Teresa
And Martin Luther King.

But like everything things have to end,
So this is goodbye,
And don't forget little things add up
So what you want,
You go and try and get it
For when you grow up.

**George Golby (12)**
Harris School, Rugby

# I Have A Dream

Black and white,
They shouldn't fight.

I have a dream,
That they will smile and gleam.

They should be friends like identical twins,
It's not what their skin colour is,
It's who you like,
Whoever your friends are,
Stand by them, and they will stand by you,
Appreciate we all have different faces,
All people are good,
They are just waiting for you to go and meet them,
And make some decent friends.

**Ross Wigley (13)**
Harris School, Rugby

# Imagine

Imagine knowing when you step out of your door,
                         you'll get beaten up,
Imagine no one to tell you it's alright,
Imagine no one to hold you tight,
Imagine knowing your family will hurt you
                if there is not enough money.

Look around and you will see,
What people do for different things,
How people will be mean,
Look around you and you will know,
What people do for money.

Imagine, locked in a cell when it's light,
Imagine, whipped forever when it's night,
Imagine, to live in fear,
Imagine, to live in fear.

**Gemma Dez-La-Lour (11)**
Harris School, Rugby

# I Believe/I Adore

My friends are amazing,
They are the best I've ever had,
They make me smile when I'm sad,
That's why I look up to them,
My family are awesome,
They are the best I've ever had,
I wouldn't change them for the world,
That's why I look up to them.

I would like to achieve a good job
When I am older,
I have to work hard at school,
To achieve the grades I need,
To make my family proud.

**Rachel Dormon (13)**
Harris School, Rugby

# I Have A Dream

I have a dream that my children will have a good life,
I have a dream that my children will never touch a knife,
I have a dream that the world will stop all badness,
I have a dream that no one will judge the way people look,
I have a dream that my family will be happy,
I have a dream everything will be fine,
Stop all evil in the world,
Say no to drugs and abuse,
Say no, don't be afraid to say no,
You can say no to anything,
I have a dream that there is love and happiness,
I have a dream that all families will stay as one,
I have a dream that I suddenly woke up from,
I had a dream I stayed in school,
I had a dream, a dream that came true!

**Thomas Jeffs (12)**
Harris School, Rugby


# I Have A Dream

I have a dream,
That everyone has the same amount of money
And is equal to everyone.

I have a dream,
I hope you see what I see,
I hope everyone can be one big happy family.

I have a dream,
To see my family not fighting,
But hugging and my family safely home.

I have a dream,
That black and white will not fight,
But see the light.

I have a dream that I am a new person.

**Matt Gibbs (14)**
Harris School, Rugby

# I Have A Dream

I have a dream to become the President,
And stop world hunger,
And stop the wars,
I want to have the mental power to end it all,
To save the people from abuse and neglect,
I wish I were Superman,
So I could stop crime,
I wish the homeless could have warm food
And a shelter to keep them warm from the cold
And clean clothes to wear,
I wish I could help the old and sick,
I want to stop ageing and the sick from getting ill,
I hope black and white could live in peace,
And stop racial discrimination,
I have a dream.

**Jamie Nicol (14)**
Harris School, Rugby


# My Idol - Richard Branson

R ich beyond my wildest dreams,
I  aspire to be like him,
C aring about other people,
H aving a great time,
A s he goes along his daily business,
R eaching out to many charities,
D yslexic, just like me,

B rave to try new things,
R ecord shops was how he started,
A chieved so much more,
N ever let anyone hold him back,
S tarted the Virgin group,
O pportunity maker for others,
N ever stops giving.

**Daniel Burley (12)**
Harris School, Rugby

# Imagine

Imagine
Being the centre of attention,
Imagine
The whole world looking at you,
Imagine
Being the only one in the universe,
Imagine
Being anything you want to be,
Imagine
Having everything you want,
Imagine
Having nothing to eat or drink,
And now
Imagine
The people that have nothing at all!

**Liliana Modego (13)**
Harris School, Rugby

# I Have A Dream

I have a dream about many a thing,
Of castles, of dragons, of queens and a king,
Or a beautiful blue summer's sky,
In which I fly, I glide, and soar really high!
Sometimes I dream of my family at home,
Where my mum's a teapot, and my dad's a comb.

I even dream of my life to come,
Of my family, my pets, my job and my son,
But really a dream isn't just at night,
If you think or imagine, one will come into sight!
Or a dream could be a trick of the mind,
(You can't help them, it's your brain being unkind),
So just expect a dream at any time of day,
Just don't let your imagination run away!

**Kirsty Garland (13)**
Harris School, Rugby

# Dream To Play Football For Manchester United

Touchline shouting, that's all I ever hear,
I'm so confused and filled with fear,
I'm only thirteen years old and football should be fun,
But with all this noise, I don't know which way to run,
'Get back in defence!' my manager shouts,
Dad shouts, 'Get up front and deal with those louts!'
Loudmouth supporter, who knows all the rules,
(He takes the rest of us for fools),
Shouts, 'What are you doing lad? Your head's in a spin!'
Is it any surprise, with this entire din?

I am only a boy, so why do you all try to destroy,
What I'd love to enjoy?

**Jack Allman (13)**
Harris School, Rugby

# I Have A Dream

I have a dream,
A dream that would change the way of the Earth,
A dream that would make people peaceful,
A dream that would make lives feel better not worse.

I dream of people living their lives,
Lives of accomplishment, reflection and pride,
Lives that were lived to the full,
Lives where all traces of fear will subside.

I dream of peace throughout the planet,
No hearts would be broken,
No guns would be fired,
No ships would be sunken.

One life, live it. Dream for the best.

**Laura Beck (12)**
Harris School, Rugby

# I Have A Dream

I have a dream,
That all people black and white,
Fat or slim,
Tall or small,
I have a dream,
That we will all live in peace and harmony,
No disgusting language,
No more despicable comments,
I have a dream,
That all people will think of each other as equals,
Even homeless people will be equal with people with homes,
I have a dream,
That everyone will be classed as one,
That is my dream.

**Brandon Woodcock (13)**
Harris School, Rugby

# I Have A Dream

Blacks and whites together forever,
Blacks and whites together forever,
Wouldn't that be nice?
LOL,
For all the pain and suffering,
We bring between our countries.

I wish we could forget it,
All our nasty comments.

What about our kids? They'll want to be like us,
What about our kids? They'll always take after us.

We'd best not be like this in a few years time,
We'd best not be like this 'cause it'll turn to a crime.

**Josh Needham (13)**
Harris School, Rugby

# Dreams

Everyone has a dream,
To be a teacher is not my dream,
To be a stuntman is someone else's dream,
To be a games designer is my dream,
Everyone has a dream,
But the world needs a dream,
I love its dream,
We can all help with that dream,
But first chase your dream,
We can all accomplish our dreams,
You've just got to want it.

**Daniel Hetherington (13)**
Harris School, Rugby

# I Have A Dream

I have a dream,
For people not to fight,
For people to be the same,
So they are not left out of groups,
I hope that homeless people have a home,
To go to at night,
I have a dream,
That homeless people have food,
And children are treated like they should be,
And are not treated like a punch bag.

**James Isom (14)**
Harris School, Rugby

# I Had A Dream

That all wrongs would
Become rights,
That all mistakes could
Be undone,
That all words could
Be taken back,
And all enemies could
Be friends,
But of course it was a dream
And now it's a *wish!*

**Rory Evans**
Harris School, Rugby

# I Have A Dream

I have a dream,
I want to sing,
I have a dream,
About Martin Luther King,
He solved most problems,
He helped people through their lives,
He even stopped most people being aggressive, using knives,
People look up to him because he is the best . . .
Martin Luther King.

**Lauren Winton (12)**
Harris School, Rugby

# Dreams To Change The World

I have a dream of a world that is faultless,
Don't have drugs, they'll make you addicted,
Don't smoke, it destroys your heart and lungs,
I have a dream of a world that is excellent,
Don't litter, put your rubbish in the bin,
I have a dream of a world that is pleasant,
Don't cut down forests, it destroys animals' habitats,
Stop polluting the world, it's killing animals,
I have a dream of a world that is unbeatable.

**Euan Prentice (12)**
Harris School, Rugby


# I Have A Dream

I have a dream that people shouldn't be mean,
People should always be kind and never have to look behind to see
If people are being mean,
I have a dream that people should be friends
And never leave anyone out,
And people shouldn't call people names,
I have a dream that people should help each other,
They shouldn't fight,
They should be at peace every night.

**Phoebe Pettifor (12)**
Harris School, Rugby

# I Have A Dream

I had a dream,
I held onto it tightly,
I clung to it too much,
Because it smashed
Into a million pieces,
And all that remained was a shard in my hand,
Of the dream that was once,
And all that remained then,
Was a broken dream.

**Abbie Hands (13)**
Harris School, Rugby

# Chris Hoy

C ycling champion,
H ero on the track,
R aces so fast,
I nspiration to us all,
S portsman of the year.

H oy - all the way,
O lympic gold medallist,
Y ou wish you could be him!

**Joe Deery (12)**
Harris School, Rugby

# I Have A Dream

Upon a pallid winter's eve,
And before the smouldering flames,
A single flake of pearly white lace,
Flew true and pure and untamed.

And through the harsh and acrid wind,
A vivid argent light gleamed,
And the torrid embers of the fire spread,
Within my waking dream.

**Kate Hadden (12)**
Harris School, Rugby

# I Have A Dream

I have a dream . . .
That the world is to be a happier place.

I have a dream . . .
That animals should be protected.

I have a dream . . .
That on Christmas Day *everyone* should get presents.

I have a dream . . .
That there should be enough food for everyone.

I have a dream . . .
That people should be equal, no matter what age,
Gender or skin colour

I have a dream . . .
That everyone should have a suitable home to live in.

I have a dream . . .
That there should be no jealousy in the world.

I have a dream . . .
That people should just get along
And care for the world they live in and the people living on it.

**Robert Evans (12)**
Lostock Hall Community High School & Arts College, Preston

# I Have A Dream . . .

I have a dream,
A dream of a better world.
I dream of a world where we can live together
Forever, with no pain ever!
The world is a dark, scary place,
War, cruelty, violence destroying the world we live in,
Is that all the human race is capable of?
Everywhere I look, I see despair, poverty and starvation.
I dream to put these things right,
No despair, no poverty, no starvation!
Just happiness and food being plentiful in every nation.
All I ever hear is, 25 more people killed in a war,
Even more innocent bystanders caught up in bombing.
If we can't deal with our own problems,
Why try sorting someone else's?
Knife crime, gun crime, abuse, sexism and racism
Clearly visible everywhere.
Can't we get rid of them?
One day we will learn to get on with others and love each other,
But if we are to survive, that day must be today,
Right now.
People are only part of the problem,
Many animals are dying out.
We need to change that.
The people responsible know it's happening,
But they don't stop it. Why?
I dream that we look after the animals,
And take care of the world.
I wish fuel wasn't running out,
And it didn't cost the Earth.
I have a dream, that others can pursue their dreams easily.
I have a dream, that the world becomes better today.
Very quickly. Right now.

**Jessica Holmes (12)**
Lostock Hall Community High School & Arts College, Preston

# I Have A Dream . . .

I have a dream for the world to be free of crimes and deaths,
I hope the war will come to an end
To save people from harmful deaths.
I have a dream for bullies to come to their senses and go away.

I dream the world could have a great personality
And people should try to save the world.
I dream that the credit crunch could go away
So we can all have brunch on Sunday.

I have a dream for the world to have faith in themselves,
And to be proud of how they look,
Whether they're ugly or gorgeous,
They still have looks.

I dream that everyone could save the animals
From becoming extinct,
I dream that people would care for the world
So we can have a better summer, instead of grey skies.

I dream that all the homeless people in the world
Should have homes,
I also dream the poor people in the world could have some money for food
and shelter.

I dream that cruelty to children and animals would come
To an end, as well as no more testing products on animals.
I hope to see smiles on everyone's faces,
Especially the doctors and nurses.

And lastly, but definitely not least,
I hope to be rich and famous (but doesn't everyone?)
And of course I'd spend the money on shoes and clothes,
But I would still do my fair share for the world out there.

**Marie Hayton (12)**
Lostock Hall Community High School & Arts College, Preston

# I Have A Dream . . .

I have a dream
To be money-free,
To have all the things
That mean a lot to me.

Generosity at my door
All these things and
Much, much more!

I had a dream
To sail the seas,
Hoping not to get the fees.
Sadly, this was only
A fantasy.

I had a dream
To fly a plane,
Sadly, this was all
In vain.

All these things have
Been and gone,
Gladly they have all
*Shone!*

**Clare Wiggans (12)**
Lostock Hall Community High School & Arts College, Preston

# I Have A Dream

I have a dream to be a superstar
With fame and fortune at my door,
Golden jewels
And killer heels
Are all I need and more.

I have a dream about a world,
A world in which you see
No disasters,
No poverty,
No more wars beginning,
No people living on the streets,
No drugs or bullying,
Just everyone living in peace.

I have a dream
That might come true
But all I need
Is help from
*You!*

**Rebecca Maddox (12)**
Lostock Hall Community High School & Arts College, Preston

# I Have A Dream

I have a dream that
I have all the chocolate in the world
And I will never be fat.
I have a dream that
I will have all the money in the world
And it will never run out.
I have a dream that there is no school but I will be
Educated.
I have a dream that
I can take all racism away
And there are no bullies.
I have a dream that
You can live forever and
Never die.
I have a dream that
Teachers are always happy
And never every grumpy.

So that's my dream!

**Chloe Woods (13)**
Lostock Hall Community High School & Arts College, Preston


# I Have A Dream

I have a dream . . .
There is no school . . .
Chilling at home would be so cool.

Playing, eating all day long,
Listening to my favourite songs.

After a while it would get boring,
Then I'd just keep on snoring . . .

Now I wonder if school is fun,
No, not at all,
Think of the homework that has to be done . . .

**Louis Enion (12)**
Lostock Hall Community High School & Arts College, Preston

# I Have A Dream

I have a dream
For the world to be a happier place,
For the world to be a more peaceful place,
For everyone to have a smile on their face.

I have a dream
For the world to be free of wars,
For the world to be free of crime,
For the world to be free of poverty.

I have a dream
For everyone to have a home,
For everyone to have clean water,
For everyone to have money.

I have a dream
For the world to be a happier place,
For the world to be a more peaceful place,
For everyone to have a smile on their face.

**Amy Benson (11)**
Lostock Hall Community High School & Arts College, Preston


# I Have A Dream

I have a dream
Everyone is happy
There is no violence
Everyone has three wishes
Homework isn't invented
And everyone is born smart.

There's no hunting
There's no littering
Nobody lies
Everybody respects one another
And everybody is peaceful
Everybody has super powers.

**Nathan Arrowsmith (11)**
Lostock Hall Community High School & Arts College, Preston

# I Have A Dream . . .

I have a dream
That the world is made of sweets
And chocolate
That everybody can eat.

I have a dream
That there is no money
So everybody has food
And places are happy and funny.

I have a dream
That there is no school
Everybody can stay at home
And that should be the rule.

I have a dream
That everybody has a friend
Who will stick with you
Until the very end.

**Alice Caunce (12)**
Lostock Hall Community High School & Arts College, Preston

# I Have A Dream . . .

I   have a dream . . .

H  ouse tax is free
A  nd all the things I buy for me
V  ery happy place to live
E  verybody shares and everybody gives.

A  lso I have a dream

D  irty water should be clean
R  ed Nose Day, you should donate
E  veryone deserves to feel so great
A  nd at the end of the poem, you will see . . .
M  y dreams mean a lot to me!

**Taylor Love (11)**
Lostock Hall Community High School & Arts College, Preston

57

# I Dream

I dream of better ways,
Of how this generation
Tends to behave.

I dream of peace,
For the war to stop,
For the killing to cease.

I dream of a clean world
With no litter to be seen,
With no rubbish to be hurled.

I dream of the education
That one child could achieve,
With belief and salvation.

I dream of a world far away,
If everyone made a difference
We could become that world, starting today!

**Jodie Straker (12)**
Lostock Hall Community High School & Arts College, Preston


# I Have A Dream

I have a dream that everyone
Can be happy.
I have a dream that no one
Will be snappy.
I have a dream that everyone
Gets along.
I have a dream that no one does wrong.

Chocolate for breakfast,
Cake for tea,

And that would be
*The dream*
For me!

**Hollie Griffith (12)**
Lostock Hall Community High School & Arts College, Preston

58

# I Have A Dream . . .

I have a dream
Of a new world
Of life and love,
Of togetherness and unity,
I have a dream.

Where children play
And mothers laugh,
Where we frolic and dance
And sing each day.

Where poverty is a thing of the past
And the young no longer die so young,
Where wars and bombs are tucked away
And the things we love just last and last.

This is what I wish would be,
So won't you come and dream with me?

**Sindy Walia (12)**
Lostock Hall Community High School & Arts College, Preston

# I Have A Dream

I  have a dream

H  aving everything you wanted
A  nd no one being left out.
V  aluables are yours and shouldn't be stolen
E  verything is fantastic.

A  nother dream that I have

D  reaming that bad things are good,
R  uling the world is this dream,
E  verything is great,
A  lways friendly faces,
M  y world is much better.

**Charlotte Mansfield (11)**
Lostock Hall Community High School & Arts College, Preston

# I Have A Dream

I have a dream
A dream of a land of chocolate and pancakes
This world is fantastic
Where there's no money, everything you want grows on trees
There are other things too
No war or suffering
Presents every day
Everything's free and there's no violence
No more school or work
No more taxes or payment
Everyone in this world is happy
No one is without food
Clean water for everyone
And Christmas every day
Everything in my world is perfect
That is my dream.

**Gabriel Wilcox (12)**
Lostock Hall Community High School & Arts College, Preston

# I Have A Dream

I have a dream that wars will stop.
I have a dream that money isn't important
Or that everyone has some and the same amount.
I have a dream that everyone has a house and is happy.
I have a dream that there is no gun and knife crime.
I have a dream that there is no pollution.
I have a dream that everything is free.
I have a dream that everyone has someone to care for them.
I have a dream that I can go shopping every day.
I have a dream I own a mansion.
I have a dream for you.

**Daniellea McCall (12)**
Lostock Hall Community High School & Arts College, Preston

# I Have A Dream

I have a dream that the world is free of crime,
And no war for money and land,
But peace and safety all around,
To comfort those in need.

I wish everyone was equally rich,
And the world was forgiving and fair,
Maybe the world would then learn to love and care.

I dream I can explore the world unknown to us,
To see other planets and people.
This may not happen but this is my dream.

This would be a greater world to live in,
If everyone could have a special power
That suited them and helped them live their life.

This is my dream . . .

**Harry Ashton (11)**
Lostock Hall Community High School & Arts College, Preston


# I Have A Dream . . .

I have a dream to become a star,
To have money and a brand new car,
Jewels and diamonds,
Money too,
And a lovely pair of gorgeous shoes.

I have a dream that there is no poor
And that they have clean water, food and more,
That everyone has a home,
That no one is alone,
To have people that care,
And people that share.

I have a dream that may come true
But only if there's help from you.

**Georgia Madden (12)**
Lostock Hall Community High School & Arts College, Preston

61

# Change

*(An extract)*

I have a dream
That maybe, just maybe, the whole world changed.
It'd be upside down and inside out
And everything in it would be rearranged.

People would start thinking of others
They'd try to be kind.
Jealousy would be banished along with loneliness
There'd be nothing left to chew your mind.

But then I'd start laughing
And realise I'd been dreaming again.
It would take much longer than the rock cycle
For people to see value in simple things like a pen.

So if I could give you
One simple piece of advice
For you to take notice of
In your life

It'd be to reconsider your life
As being similar to the alphabet.
You can use all the letters to carve your own path
And achieve any ambitions, never forget.

Out of all the letters in the alphabet
You don't have to make words you don't want to.
Stay true to yourself
I'm always going to be me and you should always be you.

Never take anything for granted
Because there are so many people not as well off as you.
Never put yourself down if you forget simple things
Like one plus one is always going to be two.

Let hopes become dreams
And dreams become reality.
But while you're achieving what you want
Don't forget about your morality.

Remember all those other people in the world
Who feel like a rabbit being chased by a fox

While you're sat safely in your home
Trying on a new pair of socks.

You're special to some people
You're not special to everyone.
Do whatever you want
And always have fun.

**Zamzam Abdullah (13)**
Manchester Academy, Moss Side

# Think

Look left, look right,
No cars in sight?
Now look again,
Any cars my friend?
What colour is the man?
Is he green or red?
If he's crimson and you're in the road then the outcome is dread.
*Schmack! Walla!*
Oh my God, you're dead.

If you're driving at great speed
And going past a school
And if the sign says 30 miles,
Then this speed isn't cool.
What colour are the lights?
Are they red or green?
If they're green you're in the clear.
But just in case,
Slow down, your pace,
In case a child is near,
Look out! There's a child, their end is here.
They look you in the eye, face stricken with fear,
You fool, oh no! You should have listened.
The shock, the horror as the blood glistens.

**Izak Johnson (14)**
Manchester Academy, Moss Side

# Me, Myself and I!

*(An Extract)*

I have a dream
To be what I can be
Dreams are forever
So dream the truth
I have a dream
To be a star
But if my dream fails
I have a back-up dream
To just be myself
Because that's all I'll ever be
Dream or no dream
It won't change who I am
Deep down inside
Myself
If dreams are important
Don't blow them away
A dream is a dream
No matter how far
It is to reach that dream
Never give up
You dream will come true
If you just believe
I have a dream
To dream a dream
That I will follow my heart
My inspirational dream is to just be
*Myself!*
Being myself is not only important
It is my life and
My dream to fulfil that life
Just being myself
I'm not vain
But I am Important for me
To just live my life
I have a dream
A dream that's important
If my dream is your dream

Then your dream is my dream
Dreams, dreams, they are important
But what I say is also important
Don't get carried away in your dream
Just be yourself.

**Sophie Foster (12)**
Manchester Academy, Moss Side

# If

If I had a dream, I wouldn't know where to start
I wish I had a million pounds, yes I like the sound of that,
I would buy lots of food and it would make me fat,
I'd buy a car, become a super star,
I'd live in a mansion with a swimming pool,
The other boys and girls would drool
Because I had a million pounds.

I'd use the rest to start a quest, a quest for super powers,
If I had super powers I would speed up the side of towers,
I'd fly around at the speed of sound,
I wouldn't have to touch the ground,
I'd shoot lasers from my eyes and change my size,
If I had super powers you'd be in for a surprise.

I'd use my powers to earn trust and respect,
I'd become ruler of the world,
If I were the ruler of the world, it would surely be a blast,
I'd make lots of changes, changes from the past,
I'd have everything as my own,
I'd sit on a solid gold throne.

If I had all of these things, I'd be as happy as a dog with a bone.
But I don't have a million pounds,
I don't have super powers or rule the world,
But if I keep dreaming I can achieve whatever I believe,
If you have a dream follow it through forests and streams,
And hope you can get whatever you want and need.

**Nathan Tickell (13)**
Manchester Academy, Moss Side

# Utopia

I glare towards the east in the snowy mountains
As the sun rises in the purple and orange sky
Watching the light glisten off the turquoise ocean
I close my eyes and breathe in the fresh air.

I take my first step
And then listen to the white snow crunch under my foot,
And feel cold wind blow through my fingers.

As I come to the bottom of the mountain the snow gets thinner,
You can see green grass and blue flowers
Spouting through the snow
And butterflies fluttering near the ground.

I walk up to a tree
And watch droplets of water
Fall to the wet green grass

I stop
And listen
I hear nothing
But peace and tranquillity
As the last autumn leaf falls.

Then night falls
I lie on my back with my hands behind my head
And look at the bright moon and shining stars
And dig my feet into the brown perfect sand
Listening to the water brush over the shore

This is a place
A place away from noise
Violence
Depression
Sloth
Envy
Greediness
And hatred
And that's why I must keep it a secret.

**Nile Brooks (13)**
Manchester Academy, Moss Side

66

# This World

This world, oh this world,
Rejection, trials and tribulation,
From generation to generation,
It goes by.

The average family trying to make a good living for themselves,
But what about the poor,
Suffering with no substance in their pockets,
While the rich boast off with their fancy gold lockets?
None of us are perfect,
I'm not a great cook,
But it tells me in the good book
To be of good courage,
Even though it's hard to stop, discourage.

'Discipline my boy, discipline,
Humility, faithfulness and happiness,
If you have this in your heart son,
It'll keep you going like a runaway cart son'.
Simple but effective words which moved me,
If only those words could consume me,
If only I opened my heart to the words Father told me.

Fear, death, sickness, destruction
Keeps ringing in my maturing brain,
No doubt that this world . . . this planet we call Earth
Isn't going to re-birth,
But it's going to break down
With all the crippling crises and unbearable issues.

But there is someone, a supernatural someone
Who can't be seen by the human eye,
If only you could only just only open your heart to that one,
With our eyes we see reality,
But if you open up your heart and spiritual eyes,
Signs and wonders come your way,
We cannot live our lives this way,
Was the purpose of the human everlasting suffering?
But ask yourself? Is there life after the end of this world?
Time! Time! Time! Is coming to an end . . . End.

**Wycliffe Chilowa (14)**
Manchester Academy, Moss Side

# Rise And Shine

Rise and shine - it's morning time
Rise like the sun
Rise like the waves
Shine brighter than a star
Reach wide and far.

Overcome your fears
Never back down
Compete with your peers
But don't be a clown.

As gentle as a feather
As hard as rock
Durable like leather
Be one with the clock.

Give as you'd receive
Receive as you'd give
Respect is a priceless thing
Give it to get it
Never forget.

Do the best you can
250%
All the time, no matter what.

Become a better person
Expect the unexpected
Take care of yourself
Guard those you love.

Surpass your limits
Stretch yourself thin
Follow your heart
Pursue your dreams
Rise and shine, shine and rise.

**Jahsida Lewis**
Manchester Academy, Moss Side

# My Singer/Song Writer - The One Who Inspires Me

My singer/song writer,
The one I believe in. The special only one,
The one who achieved it. He inspires me. Why? Ask him not me.
Will I meet him? No, yes, yeah right?
Love, hatred, faith, soul.
All of this street love baby your heart is safe with me;
Take all of this street love.
Lyrics as smooth as sponge on your skin,
Soulful as Marvin Gaye songs as he sings.
Tears flow down my eyes like a waterfall flows down rocks
But not very slow but with a glow. How did I feel this way?
Songs of joy
Songs of hate
Songs of love
Songs of hope
Happy times, bad times.
Every time I watch him the sun comes out,
Every time I don't watch him I feel isolated,
*Lonely.*
Sad, me, myself and I, alone.
I want what he has, *can't*, got to work for it.
Feeling tears of joy I clap after every concert, *but*
I'm never there. As I sob over him wishing he was here.
*Boooom!*
The lights switch off, I'm surrounded by darkness.

He's my idol, the one who inspires me,
I'll be like him one day.
Will I will me: name?

**Shallianne Ricketts (14)**
Manchester Academy, Moss Side

# I Have A Dream

I have a dream,
Not only when I sleep
But one I live each day,
One that I love so much,
Yet too afraid to say.
Kids respect their elders,
And maybe the other way,
Where everyone is friends,
Your colour doesn't matter,
Religions bond together and
War has never happened.

Special moments never end
Hold on to them forever,
Love is around every corner,
Nobody is hated,
No rain, no clouds, nothing to upset,
*No* tears on anyone's faces,
Laughing children fill the streets,
Smiles on every face.

I have a dream,
So close to me,
One I wish I could live,
But like I said a while ago
It's just a dream
Because war has already happened,
And racism still goes on,
Religions continue to battle.
So I'm grateful for my dream
As it's a place for me to hide . . .

**Ashleigh Coleman (12)**
Manchester Academy, Moss Side

# Rose In The Wasteland

When land is waste, when waste is land,
When freedom is oppressed, when oppression is freedom.
When life is war, when war is life,
When segregation is unity, when unity is segregation.
Who will stand as a rose in the wasteland?

Earth's terra-forming fire ablaze,
The murder craze,
An expanding, bewildering maze,
A rose in the wasteland.

War terrains, exploding bombs,
Soldiers firing clips into little ones,
Innocence sings its dying song,
A rose in the wasteland.

The greatest, most ultimate utopian vision,
Where goodness flows, a never-ending repetition,
If life was ever so simple, but no,
I wait, for a rose in the wasteland.

The propaganda is blatant, without a care,
The people are dying, the people are scared,
To oppose the opposition is the ultimate dare,
Who claims to be the rose in the wasteland?

With all the lies, darkness and deceit,
The liars, the murderers, the thieves, the cheats,
They rob and kill, they own the streets.
Beneath the chains of world destruction
There will come, a rose in the wasteland.

**Naim Ahmed (14)**
Manchester Academy, Moss Side

# Life, The Real Problems

Becoming a teenager has made me think of my life,
I won't always be in school,
I won't always know my best buds
And a change is definitely going to happen.
The things I take for granted now, I will beg for in the future,
I mean I won't always have people there to pay for me,
I won't always have people to stick up for me and back me up
When the pressures of life all gang up on me.

The future is coming fast
And every time I stop, breathe,
And pause this giant puzzle game,
I find out I'm late and life takes me along with it.
I feel like it was only yesterday I was screaming about being 10
And now I'm 13, soon to be 14,
And I can't wait for this crazy train to *stop!*

Every day I moan about these uncontrollable pressures
Of this giant game of frustration,
But no help,
No advice,
No nothing, all I get is
You're too young to be worrying about life,
You're too young to be depressed,
You're too young,
You're too young . . .
So what is the right age to have a problem?
What is the right age to be depressed?
I know the right age is *now.*

**Emaya Fiddler (13)**
Manchester Academy, Moss Side

# Dream To Be On That Pitch!

I have a dream to be on that pitch
To play professional footy,
My job is to play on that pitch,
I want the crowd screaming for me.

Global warming needs to stop,
Icy winters will be *hot!*
One day the world will go *pop,*
So global warming has to stop.

The two things have a click,
If the world ends
Then no *football!*
No football and I go round the bend!

My point is that my dream is football,
I live, sleep, and think about it,
Without football my mind goes split,
I dream about football.

My dream is to be a professional footballer,
That means I need to be better,
Practice makes perfect
And I'm determined to be perfect.

Whether I'm just like Aaron Lennon,
Christiano Ronaldo or Wayne Rooney,
If I'm a footballer then I'm happy,
Because I've accomplished my dream.

**Jamie Carew (13)**
Manchester Academy, Moss Side

# Stop Dreaming, Wishing, Start Realising

Here I am, sitting here, dreaming that I can go away,
Seeing my future through a telescope
And preventing the mistakes that are coming up.
I wish I had a degree in science so my dreams could come true.
I wish, I dream, I wish.

Dreaming for my favourite things,
And getting them would be a pleasing thing,
Wishing for a car or two, that would be pleasing too,
Wishing that I didn't go to school,
But seeing my friends is really cool,
Maybe without school I may have not have met these people,
Now I am glad that I did go to school.
I wish, I dream, I wish.

Having wishes leads to disaster even if you didn't mean it.
Mum goes, 'Nobody gets wishes just like that,
Working hard and getting a degree or two,
That is your effort for hard work,
Looking at the Queen who just sits there, that is her job,
So stop dreaming and wishing and start working
Because in the end
What lies ahead is for you to decide.'

**Abdirizak Mohamed (14)**
Manchester Academy, Moss Side

# You Can Be Anything

You're the star that's in the sky,
You're the apple of my eye,
You're the angel up above,
You're the one I think the world of.

You can be anything you like,
It's never impossible,
You can go ride your bike,
As far as possible.

You can be top in your class,
You can have as many friends,
You can be as shiny as glass,
You can look at life through a positive lens.

You can be anything,
Just spread your wings and fly,
Even some things in life sting,
You can carry on flying high.

Now it's time to end this,
But just remember this one thing,
Sometimes you go through hell and sometimes bliss,
You can always come out being king.

**Katherine Franche (12)**
Manchester Academy, Moss Side

# Untitled

I have a dream
That one day I will fly,
Fly, fly, fly.
If one day I will get to fly,
Fly high through the sky.

Maybe one day,
Maybe we will grow wings,
Rich ones that are beautiful,
But well-earned as well as respected.

If I had a super power
I would have wings and fly through
The sky, deep, deep blue sky
And the white fluffy clouds followed by
The horrific thunder claps, a prosperous
Yellow or blue lightning.
I wish I could fly, be the protector of the sky.

I wish
I think
I dream.

**Abdihakim Mohamed**
Manchester Academy, Moss Side

# If I Had A Million

Spend, spend, spend and spend,
I would spend all of my money just for a new trend,
I'd give three pounds to my best friend,
I don't mean to offend, be snobby, stuck up
Or look down on anybody,
I don't want to bend the rules
Or be one of those rich fools, I want only a trillion,
But that's what I would do
If I had a million!

**Aaron Tran (13)**
Manchester Academy, Moss Side

# I Have A Dream!

I have a dream that . . .
The world will be a better place.
I have a dream that . . .
My future kids will have a good life.
I have a dream that . . .
We'll help those who can't afford.
I have a dream that . . .
I could have a good husband.
I have a dream that . . .
Children won't be scared to go to school because of bullies.
I have a dream that . . .
I could fly.
I have a dream that . . .
I could give millions of pounds to the needy.
I have a dream that . . .
I could be what I want.
I have a dream that . . .
I could be a superhero.
I have a dream that . . .
My dream would come true.

**Porchya Ashworth (12)**
Manchester Academy, Moss Side

# I've Dreamt

I've dreamt of the stars beyond the galaxy,
I've seen the world beyond what we see,
I believe what I achieve is great,
I believe what you achieve is greater,
I've understood what I understand,
I've gone deep into the mind where you can't ever imagine,
I've seen the things you could never imagine,
I know things that could never happen.

My mind is full of stories, endless genres,
Playing like theatre movies,
Every night, as I slowly, drowsily go to my story world
I choose my book, my movie, my dream,
My book, my movie, my dream
Cannot be seen by even that Freddy Krueger,
He can't take away my dreams as I have none for him,
My nightmares stay with me as I cry deep within.

When real life's going bad my dreams repeat as before,
My endless dreams are unreachable.
But I'm begging for more.

**Shamyra Abbott (12)**
Manchester Academy, Moss Side

# Dreaming Of A Path To Choose

In the big, big world that surrounds us,
The small world we live in,
It's all just an imagination,
The path we choose to dream.

If we choose to dream of a world,
A world where the sun never rises,
Or the moon never disappears,
Where the dark world is in your mind,
Is this the path you choose to see?

If we choose to dream of a world,
A world where a bright future lies ahead,
Where life never ends and all is peaceful,
A world where no laws are needed,
Where there is no time for arguments,
A place where there is not any worry,
Is this the path you choose to see?

Which path you take in the world
Is the path you're meant to see?

**Alex Booth (13)**
Manchester Academy, Moss Side

# A Place Within My Mind

A place that my mind imagines is a place with no food rations,
A place that has no winter nor fall,
And in the end there is no sadness, but happiness in all,
A place with only summer and spring,
A place where the ice cream van goes *chinga-ling-ling.*

Oh, how I wish to visit a place where the warm wind blows
And the gibbous moon glows,
A place where the nightingale gives a tune
In a place where there is always June,
In the sky, there is only one cloud swirling like a ribbon
On the land there is no such thing as Armageddon.

What is this place I wonder of?
Where there are chocolate fountains that I can't get enough?
Peace, kindness, nothing but stills
With grass, trees, nothing but hills,
There I sit silent, still
Upon a green glossy hill-hill-hill-hill.

**Hamza Mohammad Hashmi (14)**
Manchester Academy, Moss Side

# If I Were Ruler Of The World

If I were ruler of the world
I'd take everything that is cold
Take away racism, take away war
Push them into a room and lock the closing door.

I'd use money and fame
To help the poor and to stop the murder
No more bloodshed or smoke filling the air
Terror but still care.

I'd make the poor rich and the culprits
Behind bars for all their sins
I'd make them suffer for what they did
And make them eat out of a tin.

I'd stop drugs and crime
Stop people from committing sin
I'd bring hope to the humanity
And punish evil doers and I would show no mercy.

**Muhaimin Bais (13)**
Manchester Academy, Moss Side

# Seasons

Winter comes with a freezing bite
The blazing wind gives the playing children
An unexpected fright.
The shining sun with no heat to promote
The pouring rain splatters on builders' coats
December comes with the Christmas snow
With an advanced style of whitening flow
Spring comes with flowers all around
Buzzing bees with their humming sound
Summer sun is now here
With winter nowhere, not near
The sun gives off a repeated heat blast
I've waited all year, it's here at last
Suddenly leaves on the road appear
I can now see that autumn is here
The trees are bare with no leaves on show
The seasons are great for I will always know.

**Birhani Nipadadae (13)**
Manchester Academy, Moss Side

82

# Rainbow

Smile, make the world happy,
It'll wake the rainbow too.

The colours that shine through the sky,
Containing everything below,
Red, for love we share with each other,
Orange, the family warmth
And yellow, for baby's first smile,
Life in green and nature,
But there are cold colours too,
Violet, indigo and blue,
The world is not perfect,
And neither are we.
The rainbow's not perfect
Beyond the big sea.

**Zaya Purevsuren (13)**
Manchester Academy, Moss Side

# Every Child's Dream!

Sweet ice cream mountains,
Hundreds of toys,
Luxurious chocolate fountains
For both girls and boys.

Rivers full of chocolate,
Hills with sweet flowers,
Trees with candy canes
And big candy towers.

Emerald glossy hills,
No one ever ill,
No need for disgusting pills,
Children playing happily in the pretty hills.

Every child's dream.

**Fatima Noor (14)**
Manchester Academy, Moss Side

# I Have A Dream of A Lifetime!

I have a dream
But am dreading it might be unseen,
Wanting to help those survive a better life
Who are in need, going back to those wars
And rescuing those innocent dying souls.
I'm not giving up at any cost,
Confidence is what I've got,
Letting go of the bad, sad, mad times
As everyone goes through them in their lifetime.
If I can be something in life,
We all can be something in life,
But to be what we dream to be
We must be ourselves within all mean,
As I also have a dream yet to be seen.

**Aneesah Begum (13)**
Manchester Academy, Moss Side

# The World As It Is

The sun was rising upon the crystal blue skies
As I saw children playing without a care,
In a world that was bright and fair
It was a beautiful day in the spring,
Everywhere you could hear birds sing.

Emeralds, gems, rubies and mountains,
Pure blue water running down fountains,
Glossy green trees,
Shiny blue seas.

Another planet, you might think,
All created just by ink.
With all the trickery and hate, it's still filled with grace,
The world is still a beautiful place.

**Fatima Mohamed (14)**
Manchester Academy, Moss Side

# I Have A Dream

I have a dream,
A dream that one day could change the lives of us all,
It will change the way we think of our lives
And the lives of the people around us,
A dream where no matter what sexuality you are
We can all walk together in the sun.

I have a dream that homosexual, bi-sexual, bi-curious
And heterosexual people
Can walk down the street with their heads held high
Without anyone discriminating against them.

It shouldn't matter what sexuality a person is
But what they are really like.
For example, if one of my friends
Told me they were homosexual I wouldn't mind,
Because it doesn't change the person they are
Or how I saw them before they said they were homosexual.

It's nothing to be ashamed of,
Life is about being yourself
And that doesn't matter what sexuality you are
Because people should be liked for who they are
Not because they are heterosexual.

Being homosexual, bi-sexual and bi-curious
Doesn't change who you are,
The only thing it changes is the gender you like.
Being ashamed of your sexuality
Is like being ashamed of the colour of your skin,
It's part of who you are.

Together we can stamp out the criticism about it
And stand up for what is right.
It takes a strong person to stand up for what they believe in,
Instead of being a sheep
And following what everyone else wants.

**Amy Langston (13)**
Queen Elizabeth's High School, Gainsborough

# I Have A Dream

I have a dream so many say,
But what does this actually mean?
I know what mine means.

I have a dream:
Global warming is an old wives' tale,
Polar bears have happy lives,
No fear of extinction.

I have a dream:
No fighting, no war, no violence,
No suffering from child or adult,
No cries of starving to death.

I have a dream:
Illness is a myth,
No tears of grief,
No scream of pain.

I have a dream:
Happiness of wealth for all,
No bankruptcy,
No credit crunch, no administration.

I have a dream:
No animals suffering,
Zoo animals in the wild,
Homes and happiness for every dog.

I have a dream:
Everyone is equal,
No one being bullied,
All the children, adults and families happy.

I have a dream so many say,
But what does this actually mean?
I know what mine means.

**Millie Broadbent (13)**
Queen Elizabeth's High School, Gainsborough

# I Had A Dream

I had a dream

That . . .
Life was worth living,
Trees never died,
Crops all grew healthy
As healthy could ever be.

That . . .
People were friendly,
They never ever lied,
Everybody always lived,
No one ever died.

That . . .
Nothing tragic happened,
Like when planes fall out of the sky,
Things that wreck innocent people's dreams
And leave us thinking, *why does it happen to me? Oh why?*

That . . .
Everywhere was beautiful,
No ugly cities or smog,
That they could all be replaced by
Lovely countryside and misty fog.

That . . .
Old and young had bus seats,
We respected our parents,
We would never be rude or talk back,
A world with no violence and no swearing.

I sometimes wonder how much
The world could cope with so much change,
It was the most beautiful dream
And then I woke up to *our* world.

**Rachael Murphy (11)**
Queen Elizabeth's High School, Gainsborough

# My Pen And Me

With a pen you can do a lot,
Having fun or maybe not,
Some words change the world,
And so does expressing them.

I have a dream where there's fun and games,
I have a dream when skies are grey,
I have a dream when I drift away
And they are mostly perfect.

I have some dreams which
Are full of crying, anger and pain,
But when I wake I realise I wasn't dreaming.

There is so much poverty but,
Some of us have none,
But really, can't you see
The government has too much money? That's why I'm angry.

I see a world where everyone is calm,
I see a world where there's no cars,
I see many worlds smiling as I see
That there's no homeless man sitting on the street.

So when it comes to helping, try asking me
For no one has complained,
I sometimes give advice or run on errands,
But in the end they are fine.

I'll give homeless food and shelter and also much more
And if this doesn't work I don't know, so please stick with me.
With a pen you can do a lot,
Having fun or maybe not.

Some words change the world
And so does expressing them.

**Jake Bowden (11)**
Queen Elizabeth's High School, Gainsborough

# I Have A Dream

Dream of a world
At school all are equal
Where it doesn't matter if you are
Fat or skinny, tall or small, black or white
Everyone is 'cool'
No one gets bullied
Everyone is the same.

I will change the world
Everyone will be equal
Everyone will be treated the same
How much I fail or succeed
I will still change the world.

Dream of a world
Where everyone gets along
Parents don't argue or get divorced
Where no one is sad from the despair
When you marry you don't stay together
For the sake of your kids
You stay together because you want to.

I will change the world
Everyone will be happy with their partner
No children will sit and cry at night from it
How much I fail or succeed
I will change the world.

Everything will be peaceful
Everything is peaceful
Bullying, children crying
Never happened,
All of it was just a dream.

**Amber Crabb (11)**
Queen Elizabeth's High School, Gainsborough

# I Have A Dream!

It doesn't matter what colour our skin is,
What shape or size we are,
There is no higher or lower,
For we are all the same.
Generation after generation we stand,
We must come together
And fight for what we think is right.

Our minds thrive for the knowledge of this,
We each carry a spark of inspiration,
Everyone is equal,
Society will triumph above all,
We must give not take,
Do not rob someone of their chance in life,
Blame others if you wish, but look upon yourself as well.

Nobody is perfect,
Everyone has their faults,
We can achieve anything,
Just reach for the stars,
Never stop trying,
Think! We are stronger together,
Nothing can break us.

Let there be no more wars,
Let us sing one song,
The hymn of mankind.
In this day and age anything can happen,
Let the dream begin,
Let us wake to new dawn,
We can change the world!

**Hannah Weightman (12)**
Queen Elizabeth's High School, Gainsborough

# Denied

I stand,
I strain,
But I cannot see,
I hear cheering,
I hear laughter,
But I can't hear thee.

This is the speech,
That marks the new start,
But I'm stuck at the back,
As if the pigment of my skin,
Changes the feelings in my heart.

I feel like an outsider,
But I can dream all the same,
Unlike my peers, my neighbours,
I don't dream of money,
I don't dream of wealth or fame.

I dream of a future,
When I won't stand at the back,
When I won't give up my seat,
When I can cast my own vote,
Not denied because I'm black.

I dream in the distance,
Maybe many years in time,
I hope I could pave the way,
For the men in my footsteps,
With skin the colour of mine.

**Sophie Hattersley (11)**
Queen Elizabeth's High School, Gainsborough

# I Have A Dream

D eath,
R age,
E vil is
A ll over but
M any of us
I n our lives will
N ever
G ive up to stop it, some will

F ight a war
O n a heart-
R acing battlefield

A gainst

B easts
E ntirely
T rying
T o
E nd lives that are in our
R eality, but

T omorrow,
O nce and only once,
M y world
O f war and
R age will be
R eplaced with
O ur
W orld of peace and joy.

**Sam Cranswick (11)**
Queen Elizabeth's High School, Gainsborough

# I Have A Dream . . . Restrictions

I have a dream,
One to change the world.
Not many share the dream,
To end the bad side of restrictions.

In life there are many restrictions,
The things that hold you back,
In many cases they are handy,
But sometimes they are bad.

Without gravity we would float away,
Though it, plus a fall, can really ruin your day.
Without friction we would slip and slide,
But it slows us down, trains and buses too.

Rules are there so we can be safe,
But they stop us doing things we want to do.
Signs are there to warn us of danger,
But danger's all part of the thrill.

Gravity will keep us here,
But not harm us after a fall.
My dream is that restrictions
Will cease to hold us back,
Friction will stop us sliding about,
But not slow us down at all,
Rules will still keep us safe,
But we will still do crazy things.
Signs could still be there to warn us,
But we would still get all of the thrill.

**Justyn Adams-Pattison (12)**
Queen Elizabeth's High School, Gainsborough

# Dreams

I have a dream that the world is beautiful,
Being kept neat and perfect like a garden.
It can be turned inside out and you can
Still pick out the beauty of it.

I have a dream that good triumphs over evil,
With the scenery of happiness and hope.
Where your feelings expand,
To love not just one person but more.

I have a dream that the princess gets the prince,
And together ride off into the sunset on a white stallion.
There, they arrive at the prince's gossamer palace,
Where they become man and wife and live happily ever after.

I have a dream that friendship and courage
Strengthens as it gets older,
From newborns to elderly,
Young and old.

I have a dream that though pretty on the outside,
The mind can be ugly and cruel.
Though ugly on the outside,
Will mean a mind of gems and a heart of love.

I have a dream which are magical things,
That show your heart's desires.
They can be powerful and overwhelming,
And leave you joyful and happy.

I have my dreams, I let them breathe and give them life.

**Megan Wing (12)**
Queen Elizabeth's High School, Gainsborough

# I Have A Dream

A hope, a wish and one dream,
The world has peace at last.
Peace for everyone,
No more fighting,
And everybody lives in harmony.

Why are there wars?
What is the point?
Is there pleasure from
Killing and destroying?
Yes, we may gain,
But what is the point
If it creates pain?

What has this place we live in become?
We should be ashamed
To call it home.
The terror we create
There, is no one else to blame?
It is purely our fault,
So let's do something
Before it is too late.

Let's stop the fighting, crime and war,
Let's stop the envy, hurt and pain.
We can't make world peace on our own,
But with your help we can make a start.
So let's change the world.

**Francesca Di Furia (12)**
Queen Elizabeth's High School, Gainsborough

# I Have A Dream . . .

People should accept each other,
Whatever size, shape, colour or race,
Everybody is equal,
No bullying, no war, no abuse, no racism.

Everybody should be able to have a clean
And healthy life,
With a roof over their head,
And a job so they can be happy.

Everyone needs a second chance,
Even if they have an illness or a disability,
Everyone feels down sometimes,
Just have fun and enjoy life as it comes.

Why can't everyone get along?
You say beliefs,
I say values, we are always arguing,
But everyone has an opinion.

People think questions have only one answer,
You're right if it's maths,
You're wrong if it's opinions,
No one's opinions are wrong.

Love your life, family, friends,
And most of all your enemies,
You have only one life,
Live it to the full!

**Megan Lauder (13)**
Queen Elizabeth's High School, Gainsborough

# I Have A Dream

I have a dream that one day far in the future
Mankind will realise what they have done to our home,
Our future is in our hands.
One day a future may come
Where we are forgiven for our bad deeds,
And that sins are forgotten,
Only we can influence our future.
Pollution is a myth of the past,
And new energy sources are found,
People shall not solve an argument with war,
No more famine or plague,
No more death or crime,
And we hope God shall help us with this.
Maybe we shall discover more planets,
Migrate to those beautiful rocks,
Understand the universe.
Hopefully we will find new friends in the universe,
And we hope they're not hostile,
We shall not fight!
We shall use our intelligence
To be friendly and kind to them,
And to ask for their help.
My dream is only a dream,
And I hope it comes true.
Who knows? Maybe it will.

**Sam Beresford (12)**
Queen Elizabeth's High School, Gainsborough

# I Have A Dream

Life is worth living,
Don't waste it,
Keep it safe and secure,
And store it for an eternity.

Love is for giving,
Share you love,
Comfort the people around you,
Even in times of misery and despair.

Change is for making,
Think of the possibilities,
People at peace, in harmony,
A changed world,
Gentle and everlasting.

Thoughts are for sharing,
Thoughts can stop a war,
They make you what you are,
So think as big as you can,
And make a difference.

Dreams make the world,
Dreams can create,
It only takes one dream,
To make a million others
Come true . . .

**Jack Cawkwell (12)**
Queen Elizabeth's High School, Gainsborough

# I Have A Dream

I have a dream,
A dream of peace, working together, man to man.
I wish I could stop wars,
There are battles out there,
This minute somebody will be dying in Iraq,
Afghanistan and Gaza.
They could be just some innocent onlooker,
Not involved at all,
I wish people would talk,
Just sit down and talk,
And compromise,
Settle their differences.
In World Wars I and II thousands were killed,
Maybe if they'd just talked, it would have been different.
War leaves the world broken,
Destruction is everywhere.
It leaves lives broken and families torn apart.
These days wars seem to be the answer to everything,
Trust me,
It isn't.
Words are more powerful than actions
My dream is to start world peace.
One day
My dream shall be fulfilled.

**Emily Towers (13)**
Queen Elizabeth's High School, Gainsborough

# I Have A Dream

To accept is to advance
A step further is a step better,
A win is not always the way,
But the spirit and a soul of fire
    To show hope in our hearts.
We must think what we truly believe,
Show courage when times get tougher
For love we show others will stay
    Look forward, start a new slate.
Do not linger on bad, but good
Do your bit to help the world
In the end the reward will come
    Imagine good in one and all.
Don't judge on first impressions
But the heart behind the wall
Is greater than all possessions
    A pot of gold near the rainbow.
See the silver lining in cloud
Stand boldly through the bad times
To be strong in heart and soul
    If change happens, what would you change?
The trees, a car, or the world?
So make a change for the better
Until the whole world becomes one.

**Ruth Lee (12)**
Queen Elizabeth's High School, Gainsborough

# I Have A Dream!

I have a dream that everyone gets along,
And then we'll know where we belong.
I wish the sun would never go down,
But you are the one, the golden lit crown.
You are the light in the dark,
That little shining spot of a mark.
You are the one who keeps the days going on,
You are the one who makes the days stay long.
When there are flowers which eventually die,
It is a sign that life has gone by.
All the people keep the world spinning,
And we are the ones who keep going and winning.
Everyone here is the light of day,
What I am for you? You do not say.
When some people are miserable and sad,
Just think of the good times that you've had.
Always keep your chin up to the sky,
And try not to ever cry.
When everyone is sad, we all become glum,
We feel small and weak like a crippled plum.
If only we were all a star,
Which travels through the sky, far and far.
Now you've heard the dreams I've spoken,
Let's just hope they're never broken.

**Olivia Lister (11)**
Queen Elizabeth's High School, Gainsborough

# I Have A Dream

When you think the world
Is against you,
It's like a bomb about to
Drop near you, only it's not,
It's worse than a bomb,
People screaming and shouting
At you, trying to hurt you.

Well my dream is for no more arguing,
Why us?
Couldn't it be them instead?
It's horrible when you just
Sit there in a corner *crying,*
It hurts. Maybe not to them but
To us.

I have a dream!
To stop violence and become better people,
Yes, people argue now and then
But you shouldn't argue over silly things.

I want my dream not to last
A minute or two, my dream is
For happiness and love.
Please make this happen, not for me, for them.

**Lily Fox (12)**
Queen Elizabeth's High School, Gainsborough

# I Have A Dream

Kindness and caring are a way of life,
Can everyone be nice or not evil?
But happy, joyful, people all respecting each other,
Corruption is another.

What you do is up to you,
If everyone was nice and kind,
The world would be lush and green,
If everyone was evil and corrupted,
The world would be polluted.

A purer world means happier spirits, times and people
As well as all kind, loving animals thriving
Whether the same, or different kinds.
Living in peace and harmony.
If all people shared one dream then this could be it.
If from a second's wish this could happen, oh, joyous days,
But it won't happen unless we all take action.

People prefer a purer world, so the next time you see someone,
No matter what race, colour of skin, hobbies,
Just greet them, be kind
And maybe you will have a new friend,
Or go away with a nice thought of happiness and care.

**Harry Wood (11)**
Queen Elizabeth's High School, Gainsborough

# I Have A Dream

Look outside, what do you see?
I see: gangsters, murder, litter.

I have a dream . . .
That there are no power stations,
Just wind farms,
That all the jungles and forests,
That once were burned, live again,
As do all that died because of deforestation,
And we (as human beings) be at peace with each other.
No war; no fighting,
Just happiness and tranquillity throughout.
No debt, no starvation,
No difference between poor or rich.
A stop to fighting is a step forward.
Racism to be stopped, is a step forward,
Everyone is equal and always will be.

I believe there is only one race,
The human race.
So let's survive as a peaceful race,
This is how our world should be,
This is the world I dream of!

**Charlotte Wagstaff (12)**
Queen Elizabeth's High School, Gainsborough

# I Have A Dream

I have a dream,
That everyone understands each other,
No one is criticised for who they are
And who they want to be.

Everyone can do what they want
And no one will want to stop them,
All ideas will be listened to,
No matter for gender, race or religion.

The arguments about football,
No one will care because it's a game,
People will support the team they like
And it won't matter to anyone.

If people want to play video games,
Then it won't matter,
Just because they like something you don't,
It doesn't mean you can take the mick.

I have a dream,
That everyone understands each other,
No one is criticised for who they are
And who they want to be.

**William Banks (13)**
Queen Elizabeth's High School, Gainsborough

# I Have A Dream

I have a dream,
War solves nothing,
Only proves who's the best army,
Talking something out solves everything,
Whether it's an argument with friends or World War II,
World peace - stops fighting.
World peace - creates goodness.

I have a dream,
Racism solves nothing,
No one cares about the colour of your skin,
Whether you're black or white, it doesn't matter,
Together, black and white can succeed,
Appearance is nothing,
What's inside counts.

I have a dream,
Drugs solve nothing,
You become addicted, depressed and poor,
Whether it's Class C, Class B or even Class A,
With no drugs comes success,
Who knows what will be eventually achieved!

**Josh Allenby (12)**
Queen Elizabeth's High School, Gainsborough

# I Have A Dream

I have a dream that all people
Will accept other people's different ways of life and ideas,
Muslims are Muslims and Jews are Jews
And people will respect each other for what they are,
Not for what they appear to be.

I have a dream that fighting and discord
Will be faded into nothing
And tranquillity and peace shall remain,
That everyone, the entire world, will be united and equal,
Let this dream come true!

I have a dream that my children, my grandchildren
And my great-grandchildren will live in a world less violent,
Panic-stricken and murderous than the one we live in today.

I have a dream that will change the world,
The places we live in
And could turn our entire lives upside down,
Baffle even God himself
And make the world a better place.

I have a dream today!

**James Harrod (13)**
Queen Elizabeth's High School, Gainsborough


# I Have A Dream

I have a dream where all war disappears,
Where the world holds hands
And agrees on everything.
I have a dream where marriage is a choice
That everyone around the world can make
And where they live free.
I have a dream where hunting for materials is banned,
And only common fish are hunted,
And I have an important dream where politics is fairer.

**Charlotte Wilson (12)**
Queen Elizabeth's High School, Gainsborough

# I Have A Dream

I have a dream
Of everyone living
In perfect harmony.

I have a dream
That there will
Be no racism.

I have a dream
Of no one to be
In poverty.

I have a dream
That the human race
Will reach new heights.

I have a dream
That there will be
No wars.

I have a dream
To have world
*Peace.*

**George Padley (12)**
Queen Elizabeth's High School, Gainsborough

# I Have A Dream

I have a dream,
That the world
Is full of music.

Everyone has an instrument,
Whether it's piano, drums, violin,
Or even the voice.

But everyone plays,
All at the same time,
Being civil for a change.

Working together,
Showing that everyone
Is equal and unique.

Everyone together,
Ruling the world,
And helping compose music.

Making the world peaceful,
Making the world calm,
Making the world co-operate.

**Amy Mackenzie (12)**
Queen Elizabeth's High School, Gainsborough

# I Have A Dream

I have a dream,
That one day the world will be clean,
That the world will be healthy,
That nothing will be tormented for its shape, size or colour.

I have a dream,
That life will be free,
That the world will be naturally beautiful again,
That everyone will be equal
And that children will have rights.

I have a dream,
That the news will be clear,
That you can say what you want, what you need
And that nothing will kill for nothing.

I have a dream,
That animals will be free to roam,
That the air will be clean,
That plants will have room to breathe and grow.

I have a dream . . .

**Beth Simpson (13)**
Queen Elizabeth's High School, Gainsborough

# I Have A Dream

I have a dream where every human being
will walk as one together,
Where no one is discriminated for who they are
And what they do
And what path they choose to take in life.
In my dream homophobia does not exist
And no one is victimised or cut off from anyone else.
Everyone is unique, different from each other
And no one should be alienated for that.
May songwriters be allowed freedom
To use dialect in which they can express themselves clearly,
And clothes designers should not be afraid
Of showing their creative sides.
Imagination has no limits and should not imply
Anything about anyone unless they want it to.
We are all unique, and we must use communication
To understand the people behind our masks.
It's not about the gender,
It's about the love that keeps us moving together.

**Joanne Johnson (13)**
Queen Elizabeth's High School, Gainsborough

# I Have A Dream: A World Of Peace

I have a dream,
A world of peace and justice,
All wars finished,
All families reunited for one cause,
Mourning their loved ones.

With a pen, the mighty pen,
All this could be achieved.

But with the pen, the mighty pen,
The world could be a better place,
A place of happiness and love,
Not anger and hate.

Anger, spite and hate, such unruly things,
Why not go for happiness and peace?

Nobody knows how much you love your family,
Well, me and my sister are a different matter,
But I love them still, more than they can imagine.

**Jonathan Wilson (11)**
Queen Elizabeth's High School, Gainsborough

# I Have A Dream

I have a dream,
To believe
That anything can happen.

To believe . . .
That wishing on a shooting star
Can change the world forever.

To believe . . .
To wish down a wishing well
Dreams can come true.

To believe . . .
That anything you believe
You'll be able to achieve.

All dreams
All ambitions
All wishes
Can come true for you.

**Lucy Lumsdale (12)**
Queen Elizabeth's High School, Gainsborough

# I Have A Dream!

I have a dream that the world will never end,
That the sun will never go down and no one will ever frown.

I have a dream that there will never be pain
And no one will ever feel ashamed.
That there is no smoking, no drugs, nothing to harm us.

I have a dream there will be no violence, no wars,
And everyone will stick by the laws.

I have a dream we are all treated the same,
No matter the colour, the height, the weight, the name.

I have a dream there will be no more crime
And that I can get rid of hate, loss, pain, time.

I have a dream we will all work together,
That everyone will be happy, no matter the weather.

But I have to remember this is just a dream,
But imagine how nice it would seem if this wasn't just a dream.

**Hannah Leek (12)**
Queen Elizabeth's High School, Gainsborough

# I Have A Dream

Pollution is cancelled
No more killing birds
No more dirty water
No more scattered rubbish.

African people are healthy
No more starvation
No more drinking dirty water
No more preventable diseases.

Cancer is terminated
No more victims
No more chemotherapy is needed
No more grief.

Black or white, it doesn't matter,
Short or tall
Bald or not
I have a dream.

**Edward Cooke (12)**
Queen Elizabeth's High School, Gainsborough

# I Have A Dream

I have a dream,
Words to change the world,
Speeches making us think twice,
Quotes giving us thoughts.

I have a dream,
A world where all are equal,
A world of imagination,
A world of happiness all around.

I have a dream,
Where people live in harmony,
No war, no hate, no cheats,
And all are the same.

I had a dream,
That people changed the world,
They pointed us in the right direction,
They changed us all.

**Harry Furnish (11)**
Queen Elizabeth's High School, Gainsborough

# I Have A Dream

I have a dream,
I have a dream,
That one day
War will cease
For all eternity.

I have a dream,
That maybe during a fierce battle,
Enemies may lay down their arms
And embrace each other.

I have a dream,
That young children
Will be able to live without fear
Of war.

I have a dream,
My dream,
A dream of peace.

**Ryan Cocking (13)**
Queen Elizabeth's High School, Gainsborough

# I Have A Dream

I have a dream,
There shall be no wars,
No deaths over who owns what,
Guns wiped out.

There shall be no poverty,
Where people can afford a hearty meal,
They shall live a life of normality,
So they don't have to sleep on the cold, hard streets.

Bullies will be a thing of the past,
Not the present.
It's not acceptable to control someone,
In such a way it destroys their life.

Freedom and praise is the road we shall take,
Respect the things around you,
Our world will become a better place,
For all.

**Max Shillam (12)**
Queen Elizabeth's High School, Gainsborough

# I Have A Dream

I have a dream,
Of a happy world,
Where everywhere you look there's smiles.

I have a dream,
Of a together world,
Where nothing breaks your circle of trust.

I have a dream,
Of a friendly world,
Where there are no bullies, just friends.

Just think how you can make a better world,
Somewhere to be walking proudly down the street,
Somewhere to be yourself, no matter what others think.

How can you inspire others and help this world?

What's your dream?

**Lily Dennison (13)**
Queen Elizabeth's High School, Gainsborough

# I Have A Dream

I have a dream that people of the Earth
Will stop polluting it.

I have a dream that I win 1 million pounds,
A hot tub and a motorbike.
I have a dream that Beanos are free
So I can read them all.

I have a dream that my little sister will
Be less evil and stop hitting me.

I have a dream that homework isn't
Given every night.

I have a dream that lessons are more fun
So I will not fall asleep all the time.

**Tristan Kemp (11)**
Queen Elizabeth's High School, Gainsborough

# I Have A Dream

Imagine a life with no marine-life death,
Dolphins and whales no longer trapped in fishing nets.
They were here before and will be here after,
They will not be killed for the bad people's laughter.
You all must know their safety won't last,
Bad people don't care, they only laugh.
They will soon be extinct
Unless we all stop and think.
Cetaceans could stay in the sea forever,
But to save them it's now or never,
We have to act seriously
To save them particularly.
We can help them be free, splash and bend,
But this could be for now the end.

**Katie Brignull (13)**
Queen Elizabeth's High School, Gainsborough

# I Have A Dream

I have a dream that when I grow up,
No more vandalism shall be performed,
And that there will be no prisons;
As there will be no need for them.

I have a dream that my dog
Shall no longer latch onto my foot,
And that the climate shall be stable
And no more pollution shall ravage our world.

I have a dream that no murder shall be done,
No burglary shall happen,
No flies will be tipped,
I have a dream.

**George Cannon (12)**
Queen Elizabeth's High School, Gainsborough

# I Have A Dream

I have a dream
To live in Strathpeffer
That's where I'll be
Forever and ever.

Where the wind stands fair
And the bird's song is heard
I will be there
Enjoying the world.

So much I could do
In this paradise
Climb Knock Farell
Or visit Inverness.

Take a bus to Loch Ness
And see Urquhart Castle
See the sights of Loch Ness
And see the stone circle.

For I have a dream
To witness Culloden.

The eagle stone stands alone
Out in a valley
A great Pictish stone
Ancient in glory.

If it fell 3 times
The sailors could use it
To tie up their lines
To reach the land.

There I will live
For worse or for better
Because I have a dream
To live in Strathpeffer.

**Arthur McLaughlin (13)**
Queen Elizabeth's Hospital School, Clifton

# Communism: Not Quite Human

Silence, but for the soft, delicate sound
Of a sleeper drawing air,
Darkness, save the pale glow,
Seeping in from the corners of the blinds,
No one stirs, nothing moves,
Yet still something great is there,
A whole new world is in this place,
It's in the sleeper's mind.

He's dreamed an Earth; yes, he's given birth,
To a world where all is true.
Where life is fair and no cupboards are bare,
Where *all* know what they must do,
Where *together's* the word, and injustice absurd,
Where everyone follows the code.
Where *nobody* lies, and *everyone* tries, *all together!*
They share the load.

Perfect it seems as the blue sky stands,
Over people all moving *as one,*
*Teamwork* is key, as with unity
They work in the summer sun,
*No one* frowns, *all* wear passive smiles,
Not one man seems out of place,
But all the while you can't help but think,
*Is this really the human race?*

And as this thought casts shadows of doubt,
This wonderful world starts fading out,
Back into nothing but a dream,
Washed away in running streams,
From gold to dust from dust it steals
Into hopeful, wishful, *false!* ideals.

**Zak Tobias (14)**
Queen Elizabeth's Hospital School, Clifton

# I Have A Dream

I have a dream,
A dream to think, feel and touch,
But when dreams feel close,
They are but far away.
The more you think,
The more you realise just
How far away they are.

I have a dream,
But when you get it,
You want more.
But what more could there still be?
And could it be so special?
And just as easy?
But what you have to do is cherish,
For dreams don't last forever.

I had a dream and it isn't until it's gone,
That you realise what you've missed,
For it only comes once, and
When it does, it seems
To also go so quickly, and it's not
Hard to miss it, for as the camera flashes,
So can time, precious time, the time needed.
But my dream isn't gone, it could
Reappear and when it does, I'll be waiting,
Watching and thinking.
Thinking I have a dream.

**David James (14)**
Queen Elizabeth's Hospital School, Clifton

# I Have A Dream

I have a dream that when I grow up
My children will live in the utmost safety wherever they go,

I have a dream that they will be accepted as equals
No matter what they are like or who they are,

I have a dream that they will be kept well away from drugs,
Alcohol and cigarettes.

I have a dream for hating to cease
And for love to grow majestically over the wrath of ignorance,

I have a dream that guns and knives will quickly become
A thing of the past and all living souls can live harmoniously
As one big family.

I have a dream of racism and injustice
Being hastily removed off the face of the Earth,
And that the ignorant minority that discard this simple rule
Will be banished from society.

I have a dream that we will never be in that position,

I have a dream that you will dream these things too,

That is my real dream.

**Christopher Andrews (14)**
Queen Elizabeth's Hospital School, Clifton

# I Have A Dream

I have a dream that one day the world will be at peace,
And that all fighting will cease.
I have a dream that all racism will terminate,
For it is something that I hate.
I have a dream that we will catch Al Qaeda,
So that we'll be the terrorism winner.
I have a dream that we'll solve global warming,
And then we'll be the real king.
I have a dream that England will win the Cup,
And not lose badly or slip up.
I have a dream that child slavery shall be abolished,
And all slave dealers will be banished.
I have a dream that freedom of speech shall be enforced,
So that everyone has their say unforced.
I have a dream that the world will be happy,
And that no one shall be unhappy.
I have a dream that we will be defeated,
By technology and robots who will be dreaded.
I have a dream that poor Maddy will be found,
And that she hasn't been buried or drowned.
I have a dream!

**Will Hammond (14)**
Queen Elizabeth's Hospital School, Clifton

# Just A Thought

I wish that one day soon,
The whale need not fear the harpoon,
The tigers of Bengal,
Would not have to fear poachers at all,
And on African plains where rhinos are born,
There is nobody killing them for their horns.

I hope that before it is all too late,
Man will learn to accommodate,
The world and environment around him, not his money coming in,
Because we expand and grow,
Animals find themselves with nowhere to go.

But I know one day my wish will come true,
Even if we carry on as normal as we all do,
Because these animals will have been killed and cease to exist,
This will stop their suffering, which is why I persist,
It is just a shame if it comes to all their deaths,
Humans could not have just learnt to live and let live.

**Ashley Clark (14)**
Queen Elizabeth's Hospital School, Clifton

# Free

One day I'll be there and I'll be there with my own right,
But for now I am stuck here in the night,
Cold and without a light,
And by day my body is weakened by the piercing sun,
But in the dark recesses of my mind
Memories of happiness are gone.
I drag myself through and through and stop, I do not dare,
Finally I notice someone cares,
My dream is to be free and I'm almost there.

**Maclaren Harper (14)**
Queen Elizabeth's Hospital School, Clifton

# Equality

I have a dream there'll be no poverty,
Where everyone can be happy and free,
Global warming won't be a concern,
We've made our mistakes so now we should learn,
The worst diseases will no longer kill,
As cures will be found for those who are ill,
Animals won't be killed in research,
Other ways will be found where they won't be hurt,
Terrorism will not be a threat,
Leaving less people angry and upset,
People will have more respect for each other,
Treat everyone like their sister or brother,
Child abuse will be a thing of the past,
So children will have only fun times and laughs,
If I could choose, all of this would be,
So everyone could be as lucky as me.

**Jack Louden (13)**
Queen Elizabeth's Hospital School, Clifton


# I Have A Dream

I have a dream
Of a world full of peace.
Is that too much to ask?

I have a dream
Where racism is unknown.
Why can't we be like that now?

I have a dream
Where medical treatment is free.
Who deserves to be ill?

I have a dream
Where nobody is killed.
How much would you pay for this?

**Josh Hodgson (13)**
Queen Elizabeth's Hospital School, Clifton

127

# A Poem For Memories

That memory, so far away
That echoes always in our mind.
But slowly it slips away,
We forget . . .
A long-lost dream, forgotten,
A great-grandmother, forgotten,
A special moment, forgotten.
But when the God high above
Takes our memories and later our lives,
We always hope that we will not be
Forgotten.
But do not fret, and take heed
When others forget, another
Will seed,
Memories are for all, and for
Those who need . . .

**Cameron Ree (14)**
Queen Elizabeth's Hospital School, Clifton

# I Have A Dream

I have a dream of a purer world,
Where poverty, racism and inequality
Have been hurled.
The white man sits with a black on a bus,
No one shouts, no one makes a fuss.
The seas, the rivers, the grounds
Are clean,
This is all part of my dream.
Global warming is no longer here,
Now there is nothing to fear.
The sun is shining down
With a gleam,
I have a vision, I have a dream.

**Theo Murden (14)**
Queen Elizabeth's Hospital School, Clifton

# I Have A Dream . . .

I have a dream that is now,
That I will stay youthful forever,
Ignorant to the perils that lie before me.

I have a dream that I will worry nought,
Sleep for an age,
Care for little,
Content in my ignorant youth.

I must be left to ponder it,
Figure out the mysteries that encapsulate it,
Whether my decisions are for better
Or for worse.

I have a dream where I will wake each morn
And realise that I have to live.
Live my dream while I have time.

**George Sawkins (14)**
Queen Elizabeth's Hospital School, Clifton

# I Have A Dream!

I have a dream,
Where we all live in peace.
No war, no battle, we all work as a team,
Everything smooth and we hold a cease.

I have a dream,
Where there are no problems,
Where we all stand hand in hand,
I have a dream.

I have a dream,
That we will all be free.
Jump, be happy,
And live in harmony.

**Bobby Naeem (14)**
Queen Elizabeth's Hospital School, Clifton

# I Have A Dream!

There's so much hatred in this place,
All because we're a different race,
People screaming, people crying,
Can't say much about the people dying.

We're all looking for equality,
Plus the fact we have poverty,
Teens using weapons of mass destruction,
While others cheer for progression.

We all talk about ridding discrimination,
Really it's another craze hitting the nation.
World leaders saying they're trying to solve it,
When really they don't know half of it.

**Oliver Samson (14)**
Queen Elizabeth's Hospital School, Clifton

# I Have A Dream

I have a dream of a better nation,
A world of tranquil happiness, that
Buzzes and hums with life and all creation.
I have a dream of cities and towns,
Where people walk without fears
And the noises of peace are the only sounds.

I have a dream of this nation,
This cannot happen without something different,
We need to stop wasting and start preservation.
I have a dream, only a dream,
We need to grasp it with outstretched arms,
To break the iron grip of our self-enforced regime.

**Henry Hill (13)**
Queen Elizabeth's Hospital School, Clifton

# My Perfect World

In my perfect world everyone's treated the same,
My dream is simple and based upon one single aim:
For men of all nations to be able to sit on a bus,
I can't really see why it causes such fuss.
One day soon, racism will finally be banned,
So now as I plead I ask for your hand.
If everyone fights for the right to be them,
We will stop being monsters and turn into men.
That's my perfect world, that one day soon,
Men of all nations will sit in a rocket, heading for the moon.
Like brothers we will laugh, cheer, and cry,
Today it's not happening, and *I don't see why!*

**Frazer Pumford (14)**
Queen Elizabeth's Hospital School, Clifton

# Yes

One small flame couldn't start this fire,
Could it?
One small microbe couldn't kill a nation,
Could it?
One small step on the moon couldn't mean so much to mankind,
Could it?
One small discrepancy in the law couldn't set a murderer free,
Could it?

Could you change the world by starting to recycle?
Yes. You could.
Could you change the world by switching appliances off standby?
Yes. You could.
Could you do something small and change the world?
Yes. You could.

You can change the world,
Even if it's small.

**Faith Tombs (14)**
St Gregory's High School, Warrington

# What If . . .?

If you woke up one morning
And everything was gone,
Your food, your money,
Your bed, your home,
Then you'd know how it feels
For those all alone
The poorest people in the world
With nothing for their own.

If you suddenly stopped breathing
And were too scared to cry
Or with a horrid illness
And trying to get by,
With no helpful doctors
To dry your tearful eyes
You'd know what it's like in Africa
When you're about to die.

If you were scared of everything
And you were torn apart by war,
Nightmares of death penetrated your sleep
Like a terrible shadowy claw,
You would not cry, 'cause no one would care
You had no friends, you were poor.
Then you would be as lonely as the poor Africans,
Living behind a closed door.

**Holly Leather (12)**
St Gregory's High School, Warrington

# Untitled

We are a family.
We all work together.
Families don't fight.
Families don't shoot each other.

If you're black or white
It doesn't matter because
We're all a family.

We sit together and talk.
We *both* stand tall.
We are a family.
We are all the same.
We all have dreams.

This is mine.

So what's yours?

Tell me your dream.
Tell the rest of the world.
Tell the other countries
Which are your family.

Tell me you dream.
Believe in your dream!

**Melissa Whitehead (12)**
St Gregory's High School, Warrington

# A Peaceful World Would Be . . .

Where no one is judged by their skin,
People are treated equally,
No man or woman is alone,
No group or nationality are targeted,
Where everyone is loved and respected,
No one is a victim or the hunted,
Life would be peaceful.

**Jack Chambers (12)**
St Gregory's High School, Warrington

# It's All About You!

Every colour, every race
Treated as equals at every place.

No threats, no teasing
Loving and happy life with your partners.

It's your choice, it's your looks
Riding, football, or reading books.

So watch your thoughts
They soon become words.
Watch your words
They soon become actions.
Watch your actions
They become your character.
Watch your character
It becomes your destiny.

No force to be something you don't want to be
All innocent prisoners and slaves set free.

If we live as one
Dream together
Our family will rule as one world.

**Sophie Cross (12)**
St Gregory's High School, Warrington

# My Dream Is

My dream is to
Stand up to hatred
Stand up to violence
And fight the war.

My dream is to
Stand up to prejudice
Stand up to cruelty
And fight for peace.

My dream is to
Stand up to genocide
Stand up to killers
And fight poverty.

I dream what I
Want to happen.

**Sophie Strogen (12)**
St Gregory's High School, Warrington

# I Can See . . .

I can see a world
Where people have the freedom to say what they believe in.
I can see a world with no wars.
I can see a world where nobody goes to bed hungry.
I can see a world where no one lives in fear.
I can see a world
Where all children have the chance to go to school and learn.
I can see a world full of happiness and joy.
I can see a world where everyone has a home.
I can see a world where there are enough jobs for everyone.
I can see a world where people are not poor.
I can see a world where everyone has friends.
I can see a bright future for everyone.

**Georgia Tyrer (12)**
St Gregory's High School, Warrington

# Untitled

I imagine with my imagination a place where . . .

We start taking more care and responsibility
For our environment, because it's our home.

A place where . . .

People take more part in things and enjoy life,
Because life's for sharing.

A place where . . .

We listen and include people, not just in games
But with opinions, because everybody's opinion counts.

A place where . . .

We don't just think of ourselves but others,
Because nobody likes a vain person.

**Christian Russ (12)**
St Gregory's High School, Warrington

# Silent As A Bird

If there was no war,
Life would be silent.
Silent as a bird in a pure blue sky,
Spreading his wings, he flies away.
He makes not a sound, the war will stop,
The day the bird flies.
Racism, fear and hatred are gone,
No pollution or global warming,
Silent as a bird. As the bird flies.

**Abbie Chambers (12)**
St Gregory's High School, Warrington

# Imagine

Imagine the world so tidy and sweet.

Imagine people having a lot more to eat.

Imagine people with a happier face.

Imagine our lives spent in a happier place.

Imagine the sky with no black clouds.

Imagine the sun that has no frown.

Imagine the world with no war or ills.

Imagine a world with no worries or woes.

**Martyn Wormald (15)**
St Hugh's Secondary Special School, Scunthorpe

# Life At War

It's dark, cold and wet here
Where we lay,
We're here with the rats
And we're forced to sleep in the hay.

We watch as the sun sets
In the distance where we glare,
We wait until the day
That we don't have to stay.

Until that day,
We are forced to fight,
We don't have our say,
We just wait until it's night.

Night is a time of peace and quiet,
A time where we can relax,
Even though the day has left many comrades dead,
I know we're all safe here,
Inside our restless heads.

**Nicole Bailey (14)**
Severn Vale School, Quedgeley

# Judgement Day

The news flashed on
As I began to cry,
Hundreds of people
Had been chosen to die.

Two astonishing buildings,
Both muscular and tall,
People gazed in shock
As they began to fall.

Hundreds of lives put to a halt,
Families have been torn apart,
But is it all their fault?

I gazed out my window
And there I saw
A tiny little woman
All widowed and poor.

She wore a black veil
And carried some bags,
Could she have a bomb
Hidden in her rags?

People ran towards her
With faces of rage
They surrounded right around
As if she was in a cage.

They spat and kicked
Then ripped off her veil
I felt useless and ill,
My face became pale.

They lined us all up
Against a wall,
Gave us a name badge
And sent us to the mall.

When we got there
They locked us in a tank,
People cursed and mocked,
My heart just sank.

For those actions of little
Nobody knew the price we have to pay,
The sorrow and anger we felt
On judgement day.

Don't blame a group of people
For the actions of few.
Make that change!

**Georgia Powell (13)**
Severn Vale School, Quedgeley

# I Have A Dream To Be A Fencing Champion

I have a dream,
To be a champion of fencing,
I have a dream,
To be the great sword king.

I can attack and defend,
And all you need to fight,
It's all about skill,
Not always might.

I have a dream,
To be a champion of fencing,
I have a dream,
To be the great sword king.

I know all the swords,
Foil, sabre and epee,
I could use all of these
Until the end of the day.

I have a dream,
To be a champion of fencing,
I have a dream,
To be the great sword king.

**Adam Davenport (12)**
Severn Vale School, Quedgeley

# Gentle Breeze

I'm flying through the wind
On a gentle breeze,
For this delight to never end
I would have to freeze.

I'm flying over meadows,
Colours green to blue,
These flowers are so romantic,
Picking one is something I will do!

I'm flying in a forest,
Beautiful nature is all around,
Everything is pleasant and silent,
Apart from running water's sound.

I'm flying through the ice caps,
Either north or south,
Snowflakes are pretty yet cold,
But I'll still catch one in my mouth!

I'm flying in the heat,
Deserts are dangerously hot,
I am sweating my liquid away,
Therefore I might pop!

I'm flying to the ground
At an extreme speed,
There is something else in the wind,
I think it is a seed.

I'm flying to my death,
My mind is completely sure,
If I pop on this seed
I will see no more!

I'm flying past the seed,
Full of happy joy,
I will live to see another day,
Another day of being a bubble boy.

I'm flying through the wind,
That horrible seed is back,
I sneeze when it hits me hard,

Then everything goes black!

I was flying through the wind,
Until I popped and had a sneeze,
I was a bubble,
So in the meadow I wish I did freeze.

**Daniel Westgate (14)**
Severn Vale School, Quedgeley

# In Pursuit

The rods are set
The reels are too,
All I want is a fish in the net,
My eyes are stuck to the water like glue.

All of a sudden the rod bends round
I don't have to wait anymore,
I'm so excited but don't make a sound,
The fish is a big one, of that I'm sure.

It comes to the top of the lake,
It looks at me,
I'm so excited I can't help but shake,
When you're fishing, patience is the key.

The fish is in the net,
I can see that it's a carp,
It splashes around, getting me wet.
I'm so glad that the hook stayed sharp.

I take the hook out,
It's now on the bank,
I am so glad the hook didn't fall out
Or I would feel like a plank.

I put him back in the water,
Off he swims
To get back to his wife, his son and his daughter,
Swimming off with his little fins.

**Cameron Ashley (14)**
Severn Vale School, Quedgeley

# The Horse Of Winter

When I was young
My grandma would come
And tell me about the horse of
Winter.

A stallion, he was,
Of the deepest, purest white,
Like new snow,
Or moonlight.

I would dream
Of his fast silver hooves,
That spread frost all around,
And then he moves.

The toss of his mane,
Scatters ice like seeds,
The tendrils tipped with silver,
Or the cold wind he feeds.

As he puts down his head,
His muscles ripple as he moves,
And with this thought,
I'm back to his hooves.

I'm caught in this loop,
Dreaming this dream,
For evermore
Dreaming about the horse of winter.

**Amy Jackson (14)**
Severn Vale School, Quedgeley

# An Individual

A single black face
In a big white crowd,
People stared
And gathered round.

They laughed and joked
At his expense,
So much hatred
It just didn't make sense.

The mocking got worse
And they began with the violence,
They punched and kicked
Until there was nothing but silence.

The violence was nasty
I hope you would agree,
But it wasn't so funny
Because that black boy was me.

They pulled it out their pockets
And stabbed me with the knife,
Now I live in Heaven
Because that stab wound took my life.

**Kerryn Taylor (13)**
Severn Vale School, Quedgeley


# I Have A Dream (Of The Summer)

I dream of a year where there is no school,
When everyone struts around lookin' cool.

Everyone seems to have an ice cream in their hand,
And everyone walks around in flip-flops
On the scorching hot sand.

The sea washes gently up the shore,
And it makes me realise I love this life so much more!

**Jessie Cross (12)**
Severn Vale School, Quedgeley

# Best I Can Be

Clap to the beat
Stamp your feet.
I have a dream to be a dancing queen.

Move those shoes,
Dance in twos,
Skip and jive, you'll feel alive.

I have lots of style
With my winning smile,
I have a dream to run a mile.

I'll train until I'm tired,
Hopefully I will never get fired,

Triple back somersault,
Run and jump onto the vault,

People say I'm the best in the world,
They also say I'm top girl.

Although my dream is to be
The best I can be.

**Jessica Wadley (11)**
Severn Vale School, Quedgeley


# Future

I want to be a teacher,
I won't turn into a creature.
I want to be a plumber,
I won't be anything dumber.
I want to be an electrician,
A job with a mission.
I want to be a lawyer,
I need to please the employer.
I want to be a nurse,
To fill my purse.

**Alice Ponter (13)**
Severn Vale School, Quedgeley

# Secrets

Every day becomes so dark,
Deep inside, tearing you apart,
I try to make a sound, a cry, a scream, a bark,
But no one cares, I'm back to the start.

Nobody knows the secrets I hold,
They all think they know me, but they don't,
All my emotions become so cold,
I can't tell them - no I just won't.

All I need to do is go,
Far away from here,
Leave behind what haunts me so,
To escape my eternal fear.

One day it will be alright,
No more fear will I have to conceal,
So I'll just keep holding tight
Until the day my heart will finally heal.

**Jessica Bond (14)**
Severn Vale School, Quedgeley

# At Six . . .

Lying in bed, all warm at night
Whilst the stars are shining bright,
The little girl cuddles her teddy bear,
Her mummy's just a minute away
Down the stair . . .
She wants for everything to be OK.
You can hear her breathing heavily, that's all
She has flashbacks of her daddy throwing
Her mummy against the wall.
Inside her heart's breaking apart,
She's been hit by a dart,
All she wants is for everything to be OK.

**Alice Cowburn (14)**
Severn Vale School, Quedgeley

# I Have A Dream

My dream is to be rich,
And own a football pitch,
Have lots of money
And dress up really funny.

I want to have millions,
Or even better, billions.
I want to own a flash car,
And also a modern bar.

I want to buy a football club
And a massive pub,
It'll be in Gloucester
And sell many pints of Fosters!

I want to be on the TV,
So everyone can see me.
I want to be on Sky Sports News,
Where sport is more important than booze.

**Peter Old (12)**
Severn Vale School, Quedgeley

# I Have A Dream!

My dream is to become a dancer,
Hip hop and street,
When I start dancing nothing can
Stop my feet.

I'm going to win awards,
Going to be the best,
Practise loads and loads
To make sure I pass my tests.

My feet are aching,
But now I've passed.
At least I have moved up a class.

**Ashton Faulkner (12)**
Severn Vale School, Quedgeley

# Untitled

My feelings for you will never end
As I love you so very much,
You send a shiver down my spine,
With one simple touch.

You are my moon, my sun, my world,
You mean everything to me,
And in my heart all I know is,
That we are meant to be.

I love you with all my soul,
I love you with all my heart,
I love you with all my brain,
I love you with every body part.

Nothing can change the way I feel about you,
I think about you all day long,
And all I seem to know is,
Together's where we belong.

**Chantelle Morgan**
Severn Vale School, Quedgeley

# I Have A Dream

I dream of being a movie star,
The glitz, the glamour and the bar,
Also the high-heeled shoes,
And the stroppy moods!
I know I will have a drink or two
But I'm through with you.
But in the end it's worth it all
When I'm on your bedroom wall.
I'm also on your DVDs
With your friends and family.
Do I still have a dream?

**Charlotte Cripps (12)**
Severn Vale School, Quedgeley

# Randomness

What would you do if a giant squid fairy came,
Jumped out of the sea and breathed a flame?
Or an electric stick man
Drew on a dam?

A hippo ninja flies through the air
Spider-Man is now a bear.
Pandas that can free run,
Gangster chickens that eat a bun.

Mutant go-go dancers
Chipmunks that are prancers.
Ballerinas that are dragons,
Lemurs riding wagons.

It doesn't make any sense
I need to get over that fence,
Oh no, someone's shooting laser beams,
Oh well, it's all just my dreams.

**Connor Williams (13)**
Severn Vale School, Quedgeley

# If I Had A Dream

If I had a dream,
It would be for the world to be at peace,
No wars
Or even disagreements.

If I had a dream,
No one would lose their lives
To useless work,
No wars
Or even disagreements.

**Charlotte Woodcock**
Severn Vale School, Quedgeley

# Dreams

We all have dreams and aspirations
We all have hopes and wishes too
We all know what we want to achieve
And what we need to do.

Some people want to be a doctor
Others want to drive a bus
Many want to style hair
Or control the traffic rush.

There are many things
We need to do on Earth
Stop all wars so no one gets hurt.

I hope you take action
On the points I have raised
To help save our world
Because it needs to be saved!

**Lydia Frost (12)**
Severn Vale School, Quedgeley

# I Have A Dream To Be An ICT Man

I   love to work, all day long.
    This job is the best
    And I always wear my bright red vest.

C  omputers are the best, I have one too.
    There is lots to do and we'll have fun too.
    Buy a computer and you might just have a better life.

T  echnology is my thing,
    And I never want to leave my precious job . . .
    When the clock chimes 6 o'clock the day ends,
    The computers are turned off,
    But one person is left, guess who . . . ?
    Me!

**Timothy Cake (11)**
Severn Vale School, Quedgeley

149

# The Paper Cow

Born from a litter,
It does not even twitter.

In its early days,
Is it eating its daily page?

When the cow is medium-aged,
Oh, it is caged!

Trapped is its fate,
That's not great.

Two months later,
Its moo was never true.

The paper cow is
Here on this page,
Where I cry in rage
Of its extinction.

**Luke Saunders (12)**
Severn Vale School, Quedgeley

# I Want To Be A Pianist

I have a dream
To become a pianist
It may seem
So hard to dream
To become a pianist.

I have to learn
How to play
I have to learn
For concert day.

Every note
And every key
Makes up part of my melody.

**Sadie Etherton (12)**
Severn Vale School, Quedgeley

# Lying On The Floor

Running round my master's house,
Keeping quiet like a mouse.
Trying hard to get away,
I need to escape another day.
Why do I deserve this?
Spending my days saying 'sir' and 'miss'.
Constantly doing everything bad,
They even killed my mum and dad.
Whipped, smacked and kicked,
From Africa where I was shipped,
Aching all over, especially my limbs,
All this for the colour of our skins.
Then I see the kitchen knife,
I'm just so fed up with my life,
They came through the kitchen door
And saw me lying on the floor.

**Ellen Forster (14)**
Severn Vale School, Quedgeley


# I Have A Dream For Peace

I have a dream for peace on Earth,
No one gets killed, no one gets hurt!

All our hopes and dreams could come true,
If we work together, me and you.

No more fighting, no more war,
No more dividing between the rich and the poor.

Thank you for reading my poem of peace,
I hope all wars will end and cease!

**Savannah Ashley (12)**
Severn Vale School, Quedgeley

# I Have A Dream

I have a dream
Of a rugby team,
They are the Harlequins,
And they always win.

They play at The Stoop,
If you're telling the truth
You'd say that Gloucester stink.

Don't support Gloucester,
Don't support Wales,
Don't listen to Kieran, he's telling you tales.

I have a dream
Of a rugby team,
They are the Harlequins,
And they always win.

**Andrew Taylor (12)**
Severn Vale School, Quedgeley

# England's Lads

A lonely soldier lay in a trench,
With nothing to fear and soon to be dead.

A wound to the arm, a gash to the leg,
With nothing to live for he put a gun to his head.

The dropping of bombs and firing of shells,
Leaves you feeling like you're in Hell.

The incurable trench foot, infested with lice,
Surviving this war was a roll of the dice.

He stiffened his arm and clenched his fist,
He had always said he would never be missed.

The trigger was pulled, his life was gone,
Another of England's lads moved on.

**Ben Munisamy (14)**
Severn Vale School, Quedgeley

# I Have A Dream

I want to be a football star
I don't want to hit the crossbar or bar.

Hit the ball in the back of the net
Oh yeah, I just won my bet.

I support England
Even though it's not a big land.

I support Chelsea
Because they're not over the sea.

I imagine it now in the Chelsea locker room
All my crowd making a big *boom!*

On a football pitch I got stung by a bee,
Oh well, I still support Chelsea.

**Michael Collorick (12)**
Severn Vale School, Quedgeley


# Monster Food

Stomping echoes through the maze
The hero's stallion runs in a craze.
Of fear and terror all must feel,
In the home of the monster meal.
That hunts the night eating cattle,
Still our hero goes with thought of battle.
To slash and rend,
For the innocent he must defend.
The beast gets closer still,
Crunching through rock, ready to kill.
The hero's sword shines bright!
As he slashes at the fright.
The monster fowl is dead,
Munching on chicken our hero goes to bed.

**Kieran Brown (13)**
Severn Vale School, Quedgeley

# A Dream

Over a sixth of the Earth
Lives on a dollar a day
Unable to do as they need.

Thousands die of malnutrition,
Starving amongst the streets,
And still more must leave their homes.

In famine's wake walks disease,
Pestilence stalks the land
With war, hand in hand,

Unless we act now.

Wars have raged for a thousand years
Leaving so many billions dead
And so few to mourn them.

And in all this
No one cares!
As long as they can reap the benefits.

Choking fumes clog the air,
It's so hard to see,
So hard to breathe!

Unless we act now.

I have a dream
That we will act now
To prevent this nightmare
Coming true,
For this is not a tale
Of the mysteries of the future,
This is the fact
Of now.

We must act now,
We will act now!

**Rory Braggins (13)**
Soham Village College, Ely

# Lots Of Children Out There

Lots of children out there are helpless and alone,
They are beaten and bruised with nowhere to go.
Lots of children out there are not looked after properly,
They go through lots of pain and suffering,
We need to help them.

Lots of children in the world are afraid of parents or carers,
They are living in danger with fear of telling someone.
Lots of children in the world are humiliated and sworn at,
They are hungry and dirty with no clean clothes to wear.

Lots of children out there are growing up in dangerous houses,
They are growing up with drug addicted or alcoholic parents.
Lots of children out there
Are not getting the right medical treatment,
They are injured and afraid, we need to help them.

Lots of children in the world are terrified to go home,
They are suffering from depression and neglect.
All of these children are going through child abuse,
We need to help them.

**Charlotte Stevens (12)**
Studley High School, Studley

# Untitled

Green is land and Earth.
Green is environmental
But environmental damage
Is happening.

People can stop!
The Earth is being damaged.
Green is going
So save it!
Keep the Earth.
Stop it!

**Matthew Fletcher**
The Friary School, Lichfield

# What's Life Like In 2084?

Electricity's not working
The wildlife is not here
I can feel something lurking
It's filling me with fear
Houses are overtaking
The temperature is so hot
It's a horrible world we are making
The landscape now has a blot
The sky is so dark
The pavement is not clean
Take a look in a park
How could we be so mean?
It could only be 2084
What was life like before?
Well
The sky was blue
There was countryside
Electricity too
There was no need to hide
The weather was great
Wildlife was intriguing
The sun was never late
People were still believing
The air was worth breathing
The world was worth living
The world won't always be the same
But it doesn't have to change for the worse!

**Tavis Taiwo (11)**
The Friary School, Lichfield

# The Environment

What does the future hold for us?
Polluted skies, black with smoke,
Litter clutters the pavements,
Cars are making traffic in the streets.

The simple things we can do to help put a smile on someone's face,
On a day, years from now where things may have changed
Like the skies which have been polluted from blue to black.

Save some trees which are slowly decreasing,
As we waste paper carelessly
Why not use two sides and save some trees?
Or simply recycling even different materials like glass bottles and cardboard
This can use less energy and pollution than making things from scratch.

How can we reduce our carbon footprint?
Let's start by turning our TVs off at the plug,
Instead we choose to leave them on standby
Or simply turning lights off when not needed.

**Lydia Bradley Lowbridge (12)**
The Friary School, Lichfield


# Pollution

Everybody shall look into the skies
With their big eyes
And see the bubble of pollution
We have made

I hope in my life I
Will see a sky so
Blue for the children that will
Follow me

A world so clean that will breathe so
Free and pollution is no more
A word in the dictionary.

**Ben Webb**
The Friary School, Lichfield

# Global Warming

Global warming, not hard to explain,
It's killing the Earth with great pain.

It hurts our planet in many ways,
We need to stop it in weeks and days.

We're slowly running out of time,
So act now and all could be fine.

We all need to be involved
So this problem can be solved.

Recycle your paper, bottles, cans and plastics,
This would help the world and be fantastic.

So, all go home and do your part,
It's never too late for you to start.

Look after the world like it's your friend
And hopefully it will never end.

**Adam Lewis**
The Friary School, Lichfield


# If You . . .

If you have cans try to recycle,
If you leave the car and instead choose the cycle,
If you are out put your litter in the bin,
If you switch off the lights when you are not in,
If you don't leave your telly on standby,
If you don't watch as the wildlife all die.

If you stop and think about it,
Then you're making an effort and doing your bit.

**Emily Townsend (11)**
The Friary School, Lichfield

# I Have A Dream

Don't you believe
You could be the inspiration?
Don't you believe
You turn people statue-still?
Don't you believe
Your words could burn like fire?
Don't you believe
Your righteousness drugs them like a pill?
Don't you believe
Your dreams can open up and blossom?
Don't you believe
The time you send pulses racing?
Don't you believe
Your words can be more than a riddle?
Don't you believe
In the heartbeats you send pacing?
Don't you believe
How your beliefs caress people?
Don't you believe
You can put right in their minds?
Don't you believe
You can bring people sanity?
Don't you believe
You can help all kinds?
Don't you believe
You can make butterflies flutter?
Don't you believe
You can roar out the truth?
Don't you believe
You can mend things in a heartbeat?
Don't you believe
You can help elderly, adults and youth?

*Don't you believe in your dreams?*

**Hannah Slaouti (14)**
The Kingsway School, Cheadle

# I Have A Dream

Isn't it time
That you see the future?
Isn't it time
That you use your mind?
Isn't it time
That you came out of the dark?
Isn't it time
To make a difference?
Isn't it time
That you inspired others?
Isn't it time
That you put pen to paper?
Isn't it time
That you thought of others?
Isn't it time
To raise your voice?
Isn't it time
To encourage the weak
Isn't it time
To open up your heart?
Isn't it time
To stop wasting life?
Isn't it time
To be a first rate version of yourself?
Isn't it time
To unlock the door?
Isn't it time
To make dreams come true?
Isn't it time
That *you* changed the world?

**Josh Thompson (13)**
The Kingsway School, Cheadle

# I Have A Dream . . .

I have a dream
A recurring theme
A theory of equality.

No upper class, no working class
'Cause we're in a class of our own
No division of people
A community of us together
Not out of need but out of humanity
No longer the clash of private property
Because property is not ours, it is property's.

Freedom from the concrete walls of segregation, fascism, chauvinism, and
The iron bars of phobia, control and hate
That make our prison.

We may only be spectres
But our condition is not permanent
The future is not yet painted
But already blood and tears
Spread over the canvas
Not smiles and happiness which spectres are denied.

While I cry for I know it was only a dream
But I will fight with tears
For the realm I dreamt.

**Matthew Connolly (14)**
The Kingsway School, Cheadle

# I Have A Dream

I have a dream.
What if life was like a fairy tale?
Then everyone would get their happy ending.
No painful experiences, no threatening abuse,
Perfect.

Maybe one day there will be world peace,
All wars will end, people will throw down their guns
And realise they have a life to lead.
They'll shake hands with the enemy,
Perfect.

People that respect each other for who they are,
Believe in themselves, are treated equally.
I dream that world hunger would end,
Get a basket of food and share it out to the world,
Perfect.

I dream domestic violence would never happen,
No harm would come to anybody,
That everyone would find their shining star,
Their light at the end of the tunnel.
Perfect.

My dream.

**Katie Strong (14)**
The Kingsway School, Cheadle

# I Have A Dream . . .

A dream is . . .

A whirlwind of thoughts teeming through your mind,
A million images dancing and swaying to your imagination,
A pit of randomness that you cannot escape.

A dream is . . .

A hallucination of the mind,
Your subconsciousness attempting to take over,
Your heart showing you its desires through pictures and films in your head.

A dream is . . .

The past trying to escape its chamber,
Your memories trying to become alive once again,
Your emotions taking over.

A dream is . . .

Scary, upsetting, romantic, happy, helpful, enjoyable,
Your hopes and ambitions flashing before you,
A taste of what you really want.

A dream is . . .

Anything you want it to be.

**Laura Novacki (13)**
The Kingsway School, Cheadle


# Dreams

Dreams are little drops of Heaven
They're secret, you keep them to yourself.
Dreams are a fat child's chocolate cake
The magic they work up inside you.
No one's dream can ever be as good as yours.
No one can ever take it away from you.
There is always something you can say . . .
'I have a dream.'

**Amy Clouston (14)**
The Kingsway School, Cheadle

# My Dream

M agical! Amazing, magical things happen,
   suddenly there is peace and quiet,
   thoughts fill your sleepy head.
Y ou! Dreams are what *you* believe
   what *you* want to happen, it's easy,
   not hard.

D esire! All these things you really want
   are in your dreams,
   images, sounds and feelings.
R estless! You toss and turn,
   your thoughts are piling up,
   you don't realise that things are on your mind.
E asy! You don't realise how easy life could be
   if all your dreams came true,
   how happy, ecstatic, mirthful you would be.
A dventurous! Your dreams can be
   anything you want them to be,
   weird and different.
M emories! Dreams are just your memories merging together,
   turning them into something spectacular
   and different.

**Jessica Vernon (13)**
The Kingsway School, Cheadle

# I Have A Dream . . .

*I have a dream . . .*
For the world to be peaceful,
For the soldiers out there to be safe
And people not to be affected by roadside bombings.

*I have a dream . . .*
That soldiers' families won't have to hear the bad news,
That all wars will just stop
And there will be no hatred.

*I have a dream . . .*
That violence won't be the answer to arguments,
That the world will not revolve around war and money,
And for people to live.

*I have a dream . . .*
So that innocent lives will not be taken away,
For people to communicate without arguments,
For people to get along.

*I have a dream . . .*
For people to live their lives to the full,
Without being killed by a bomb.

**Jessica Conway (14)**
The Kingsway School, Cheadle


# I Have A Dream

D  is for death, the result of war
R  is for realising that we can do more
E  is for expectations, how people expect us to be
A  is for achievements, reaching your goals and dreams
M  is for money that the poorest countries need
S  is for success, if you try hard, you'll succeed.

I have a dream, so do you,
I've shared mine, will you share yours too?

**Alaina Halim (13)**
The Kingsway School, Cheadle

# Have A Dream

I have a dream that one day
Every soldier will drop their weapons
And stop fighting.

I have a dream that one day
People will see the world
And start writing.

I have a dream that one day
People will accept each other
And get on.

I have a dream that one day
Cruelty to children and animals
Will be gone.

I have a dream that one day
Fatal diseases
Will be cured.

I have a dream that one day
People who spread happiness
Will get a reward.

**Katie Inwood (13)**
The Kingsway School, Cheadle

# Dreams

I have a dream
That will change lives
Forever everyone
Would be equal
And lives would be better.

I have a dream that
All poor people became
Fortunate.

I have a dream that
All ill people would
Get better.

I have a dream that
All wars would
Stop.

I have a dream that
The world would
Become a better
Place!

**Lauren Beaumont (13)**
The Kingsway School, Cheadle

# I Have A Dream

Everybody has a dream,
Some are silly and won't come true,
But some are practical and take dedication,
And some will be forced to stay in your imagination.

Maybe they're to meet someone famous,
Become a rock star or a sports star,
Some people want to become art thieves,
They all can come true if you believe.

But some people's dreams are just to survive,
To feed their family, watch their kids grow up,
These people live in poverty,
Their dreams are less likely to be.

My dream is to help make a difference,
Maybe I'll find a cure for a deadly disease,
Or maybe I'll just travel the world, see everything.
To be honest, I don't know what my dream is.

I'm not sure of my dream . . .

**Sam Cowhig (14)**
The Kingsway School, Cheadle


# I Have A Dream

I have a dream, my own and independent dream,
I want to smell the beautiful flowers in fairyland,
I want to taste the biggest cake that will melt my heart away.

I want to touch the tip of the sky,
Letting the stars shine upon me,
I want to be under the spotlight forever.

I want to travel the world, and capture every second,
I don't want to be famous,
I don't want to be the brightest crayon in the box,
I want to be ordinary. I want to live in my own world.

**Jess Tsang (14)**
The Kingsway School, Cheadle

# I Have A Dream

I have a dream where no one can get killed
Over something that has nothing to do with them.

I have a dream where all countries
Will not have any disputes.

I have a dream where no one will be exterminated
Because they don't believe in the right things.

I have a dream where no one is shot
Because of what they believe in.

I have a dream where all diseases are cured
With one single vaccination.

I have a dream where anyone can get on an aeroplane
And not be suspected of anything.

I have a dream where all nuclear
And weapons of mass destruction are all gone.

I have a dream.

**Jonathan Rourke (14)**
The Kingsway School, Cheadle

# Dreams Are . . .

What life starts off at . . .
What you grow up with . . .
Every child's piece of cake . . .
Little droplets of Heaven . . .
The one you love . . .
What you can achieve in life . . .
What you want more than anything . . .
Golden rays of sunshine . . .
Stars in the sky . . .
A love for something pure and tender . . .
Something wonderful . . .
Something that makes your heart beat . . .
A light in the dark . . .
Something no one can take away . . .
Your final wish.

**Olivia Gibbons (13)**
The Kingsway School, Cheadle


# I Have A Dream

I have a dream of a mystical place
With fairies and unicorns,
I have a dream of a mystical place
Lots of gold but no leprechauns.

I have a dream of a peaceful place
No guns, no bombs, no war,
I have a dream of a peaceful place
With a library and more.

I have a dream of a happy place
No fighting or shouting,
I have a dream of a happy place
Where everyone's smiling.

**Joe Seddon (14)**
The Kingsway School, Cheadle

# I Have A Dream . . .

I have a dream to climb a mountain,
I have a dream to fly high in the skies,
I have a dream to stop all the wars
And bring the world to peace.

I have a dream to be rich and famous,
I have a dream to see my money help others,
I have a dream to travel the world.
*I have a dream!*
*I have a dream . . .*
*I have lots of dreams . . .*

I have a dream to help the world,
I have a dream to see
All the world's stunning sights,
I have a dream to be *powerful!*

**Tom Stuckey (14)**
The Kingsway School, Cheadle


# I Have A Dream

I have a dream,
Real only to me.
It's magic to me when I sleep,
Letting my imagination run free.

I have a dream,
To climb the tallest mountain,
See the small world,
Watch my money fountain.

I have a dream,
The same one every night,
To be rich and famous,
Forever in the spotlight.

**Rachael Morrey (14)**
The Kingsway School, Cheadle

# I Have A Dream

*(Based on Barack Obama's victory speech)*

I have a dream
To help the world
No matter how hard or how easy
Or even if this is what people have deserved.

The answer spoken, by anybody,
Old, young, black, white, Democrat or Republican,
Disabled or not disabled,
Tonight is your answer.

The unsung hero of the campaign
Who built the best,
He who is talented, brave, smart,
He has a dream,
He wants to make it come true.
We can all help to make a dream come true.

**Jacqui Skelton (13)**
Tytherington High School, Macclesfield

# I Have A Dream . . .

I have a dream
Upon a star
I close my eyes
And my mind goes far.

I have a dream
Of world war peace
Where all the sufferers
Shall be released.

I have a dream
Of a world so vivid
We shall be free
Of a world so livid.

I have a dream
Where love's so strong
It takes you down,
Is that so wrong?

I have a dream
Where kids love school
Where responsibility
Seems real cool.

I have a dream
The whole world smiles
And all the problems
Are locked and filed.

And now the dream must come to an end
I must awake and start again.

**Beth Manning (13)**
Wade Deacon High School, Widnes

# Only In A Dream

I am there falling, flying,
Laughing, crying.
I rise up through the clouds and I fall through the Earth,
I curl up and die, I see my rebirth.
I once thought my mind was sane and sound,
My thoughts were tightly, harshly bound.
Yet I broke through the boundary so swift in my sleep,
As I slept soundly my mind she did leap.
I lost myself, I never foresaw,
My dream closing in but I wanted much more.
My whole mind in dream she was reborn,
Yet with nightfall also came dawn.
I fought the light laying across my eyes,
My dream she was dying, I heard her sad cries.
I gasped for the air,
My dream, she had died, my mind was stripped bare.
As sad as I was in shock there I lay.
My dream, will she find me again some bright day?

**Hannah Dodd (14)**
Wade Deacon High School, Widnes

# I Have A Dream . . .

I wish for poverty to be abolished,
I wish for racism to be demolished.

I wish everyone could pursue their dreams,
I wish that everyone could make their own teams.

I wish that everybody could have a hero close to them,
I wish everybody could have their own shining gem.

I wish that everyone is there for one another,
I wish that everyone could trust one another.

I wish a hero could stand by you,
I wish they could make you happy when you're feeling blue.

**Sophie Moores (13)**
Wellington School, Timperley

# It's A Life To Live

Goals to achieve,
It's a life to live,

Friends one minute,
Enemies the next,
A happy family,
Constantly at war,
What a life to live.

Teachers mean and strict,
Teachers kind and helpful,
Homework all night long,
Boring. Nothing interesting,
What a life to live.

To bed at 9,
Never late,
Awake at 7,
Tired all the time,
What a life to live.

Rumours from nowhere,
Chatter for no reason,
Pressured and forced,
No one to understand,
What a life to live.

We fight and struggle
To make a change
Lead better lives,
To move forward,
What a life to live.

To live up to expectations,
To prove what we are,
That we are gifted,
That we are talented,
What a life to live.

It's hard at times,
We live and regret,
But we never waste,
A single second,
It's a life to live.

**Lauren Harrison (12)**
Wellington School, Timperley

# I Have A Dream - Animal Cruelty

*Cruelty*
It has to stop,
Before they pop.
*Cruelty*
To see cats and dogs
Being cut up, like dissecting frogs.
*Cruelty*
Many dogs being beaten up,
And then their brain stashed in a cup.
*Cruelty*
Monkeys sent away from home,
So alone.
*Cruelty*
Rats and mice do no harm,
In fact they're quite a charm.
*Cruelty*
Prisoners sentenced for life,
They should go under the knife.
*Cruelty*
How would it feel
To see your friend being peeled?
*Cruelty*
Seeing your friend
Come to an end.
*Cruelty.*
No one's there.
*Cruelty.*

**Laurel Worthington (13)**
Wellington School, Timperley

177

# War

In the world we live in today,
War is all around us,
Happening all through the day,
We live through it
And pray for the end,
Wondering where it will strike,
Do you think it's right?

I'll tell you what,
It's got to stop,
We need to change this world around,
We need to stop it,
No questions asked,
It needs to stop.

People die,
Loved ones lost,
We mourn and cry,
And pray for the rest,
Sticking together,
Death's door round every corner,
But yet we carry on.

I don't agree,
Not at all,
This has to stop,
Full stop,
I'm fed up of running,
Fed up with hiding,
Why can't it just end?

Our world is all mixed,
And we are trying to sort it out,
Some people don't agree,
And fight against us,
We fight back,
Many die,
But we keep fighting.

I believe we can change,
I believe that it will end,

Maybe not today,
Or any day soon,
But it will change,
I know it will,
If we just believe.

**Heather Valentine (12)**
Wellington School, Timperley

# What Hope Means

What hope means

Hope is bright shining light which keeps darkness away,
Hope is a gentle cold breeze on a hot summer's day.

What hope means

Hope is an oasis in a desert,
Hope is a diamond in the dirt.

What hope means

Hope is as light as a feather,
Hope goes on forever and ever.

What hope means

Hope is dreaming of tomorrow,
Hope is simmering under sorrow.

What hope means

Hope is sparkles in our eyes,
Hope is a beautiful thing and this beautiful thing never dies.

What hope means

Hope is free of cost,
Hope is the last thing ever lost.

What hope means

Hope is not mine, nor his,
Hope is what hope is . . .

**Anna Loftus (13)**
Wellington School, Timperley

# I Have A Dream . . .

To be able to see the world, able to view what surrounds me.
God gave me eyes to see, it's not all about *me, me, me!*
I only get one life so I will live it to the full,
I don't want to sit at home with my gran knitting wool.
I want to meet new people rather than just a couple of friends,
Forget about my past and make amends.
I want to climb up high, as high as a mountain,
I need to be quick to have a look at the giant fountain.
I want to see the little creatures hiding in the sea,
I will need to be quiet so they don't see me.
I want to visit Africa on a safari
And help the little children less fortunate than me.
Instead of watching the news I want to go on a cruise
And breathe fresh air and see creatures that are rare.
I want to hear a grizzly bear growl,
I want to hear an evil wolf's howl.
I want to try every food that gets me in a good mood.
I will scream, you will scream,
We should scream for a new ice cream.
I want to learn to surf and play on Astroturf.
I want to see all my history for all I know it's a big mystery!
I want to star in a big movie, I think that's groovy.
I want to ski, I want safari, I want to see a parrot eating a carrot.
I want to see the countryside and maybe even paradise.
I want to go to Blackpool with all my friends from school.
I want to go to Lazerquest and hopefully find a treasure chest.
I want to meet all movie stars
And drive around in the hottest new cars.
I want to try every sweet
And persuade people to have a little treat!
Anybody that wants to go to the moon will go *boom,*
So stay on the Earth!
I like to design but also rhyme.
If I go fast I will complete a task, if I go slow I will never know!
I hope throughout my life I will have this much fun,
I know these are my dreams, but my life has only just begun.

**Maria Neocleous (12)**
Wellington School, Timperley

180

# Do You Believe?

Do you believe?
I have inspiration,
I have determination
To make this world a better place,
So that we consider every race.

When we work together our ideas will fly,
Love and trust will never die,
We all have dreams that lie ahead,
We all hope that tears won't be shed.

Do you believe?
I have inspiration,
I have determination
To make this world a better place,
So that we consider every race.

Love, hope, peace and trust,
We all need this, we really must -
Always, always stick together,
Just like a bird and its feather.
Courage, strength, happiness and joy,
We all need this, every girl and boy.

Do you believe?
I have inspiration,
I have determination
To make this world a better place,
So that we consider every race.

We all need to believe,
We all have inspiration,
We all have determination
To make this world a better place,
So that we consider every race.

**Holly Sutton-Brand (12)**
Wellington School, Timperley

# Keep Me!

Keep me smiling,
Keep me laughing,
Keep me safe
And keep me calm.
Keep me tidy,
Keep me neat
And keep my heart rate at a steady beat.
Keep me fed,
Keep me warm,
Keep me snug
And keep me a hug.
Keep me sunshine,
Keep me rain,
Keep me clothes
And keep me a game.
Keep me sane,
Keep me reading,
Keep me cooking
And keep me sealing.
Keep me clouds,
Keep me Heaven,
Keep me happiness
And keep me sadness.
Keep me glory,
Keep me misery,
Keep me paper
And keep me a pen.
Keep me friends
And keep me family.
But one thing I ask for is don't keep me death!

**Natalie Doggett (13)**
Wellington School, Timperley

# I Have A Dream

I have a dream that everyone can read and write
And everyone can learn.
I have a dream that one day wars will end
And there will be peace.
I have a dream that no child will ever be alone
And that everyone shall have a chance for love.
I have a dream that black and white will come together
And racism will end.
I have a dream for no adult or child to die
Because there is not enough food or water for them.
I have a dream that religion won't cause wars
And that people won't die because of what they believe in.
I have a dream that no one shall die alone
Or die without being loved.
I have a dream that the bad people in life
Will become good.
I have a dream that everyone can have a second chance.

I have a dream for the grass to stay green
And the sky to always be blue.
I have a dream that no one shall die
Because of someone else's mistakes.
I have a dream for everyone to have a friend
And someone they can trust.
I have a dream for everyone to have someone to pick them up
When they are down.
I have a dream that life won't end
And is forever.

I have a dream that everyone is kind,
Caring and thoughtful to each other.

**Lily Preston (13)**
Wellington School, Timperley

# Why?

Family
Are the people we love,
Yet we fight and separate
Like two sides in a debate.
*Why?*

Friends
Are the people we depend on,
Yet the fight goes on,
To stay friends forever.
*Why?*

Adults,
Parents, teachers and many others,
These are the people who look after us,
Yet we still scream and shout at them.
*Why?*

Animals,
Part of the family,
Yet some people will just
Leave them on the street.
*Why?*

I, you, me, they,
We are all connected in a way,
We are all a part of each other's lives,
So we need to stick together
And live on with each other.
*Why?*

Because it's true . . .

**Nanami Butler (12)**
Wellington School, Timperley

# Inspiration!

Inspiration,
People who are an inspiration
Have lots of determination,
They have good dedication.
An example of this determination
Is my mum, who is my inspiration.
She never stops being so kind,
It's like she doesn't mind.
I take her for granted, I feel so bad,
But it's like she doesn't care, she must be mad.
Another inspiration is Steven Gerrard,
He tries really hard,
He has determination and dedication,
That's why he's an inspiration.
My main inspiration,
Who has all the determination,
All the dedication,
And who gets my congratulation
Is Rosa Parks,
She stood up for what was right,
Even if it led to bad remarks,
She got arrested for doing right.
She's my inspiration
For all her determination
And her courage,
To stand up for what was right,
She's a great inspiration,
Inspiration.

**Paul Ogden (12)**
Wellington School, Timperley

# Imagine A Hero

A hero could come in
Many shapes and sizes.
Imagine a hero.
A hero is different to
You and I and
Can come in many guises.
Imagine a hero.
A hero could be an animal,
Human, large or small.
A hero could be black
Or white, short or
Tall.
Imagine a hero.
A hero can be an
Artist, a writer or even
In war.
If we were like
Them there'd be a
Lot more.
From Barack Obama
To Martin Luther King
Or it could be a
Rock star ready to
Sing!

Imagine a hero,
Who's yours?

**Patrick Glitherow (13)**
Wellington School, Timperley

186

# I Have A Dream

I have a dream there will be
No more war.

I have a dream there will be
No more crimes.

I have a dream that graffiti will be an art
And not a crime.

I have a dream the world will be
A better place.

I have a dream orphans
Will all have families.

I have a dream that people less fortunate than us
Are as fortunate as us.

I have a dream that people with no water
Will have water.

I have a dream that people in the war
Will live through it.

I have a dream that people that have lost their children
Will get them back.

I have a dream that people who are poor
Will be rich.

I have a dream that people that have diseases
Will be healed.

**James McNeil (12)**
Wellington School, Timperley

# Rights

I have a dream that one day
We will all have rights, and not
One person ruling over
Another.

I hope that we will all be equal
With no one higher or lower than
Us.

I dream that we will have world
Peace and not have violence of
Any sort, no matter what part of
The world it is.

I believe that one day we will
Be able to live together as
One, as a community and in
Harmony.

I dream that one day the
Criminals will help us up when
We are down.

I believe that we are all equal.

I have a dream that one day
We will all have rights, and not
One person ruling over
Another.

**James Smethurst (12)**
Wellington School, Timperley


# My Mum!

Mums care for you.
Mums look after you.
Mums trust you.
After all they are your mum!

**Hannah Murphy (13)**
Wellington School, Timperley

# The Forest

*I woke*
To be enveloped in green
*I woke*
To see small cubs nuzzling their mother
*I woke*
Smelling the crisp warmth of summer
*I woke*
To hear the silent *whoosh* of an arrow
*I woke*
Watched by the silent observant trees
*I woke*
To hear the happy laughing of people
*I woke*
To see a young deer walk to where I slept
*I woke*
To see the world of peace
*I woke*
To see a small river flow by
*I woke*
To see people enjoying their short lives
*I woke*
To see the forest
*I woke*
To see what freedom really means.

**Bradley Mitchell (13)**
Wellington School, Timperley

# Just Think . . .

Think about the world,
Imagine a life with no war,
No hunger,
No pain,
Just think about the environment,
The animals,
The people,
The air,
Imagine a life with no diseases,
No cancer,
No AIDS,
Think about the bad things in life,
Global warming,
Bullying,
Losses,
But we,
As a nation,
Will push through the horror,
Find answers to all the questions,
Find cures for all diseases,
Find food for those who are hungry,
Find homes for the homeless,
Our lives will succeed,
Together! One nation!

**Dylan Evans (13)**
Wellington School, Timperley

# I Have A Dream

I have a dream, that all wars will stop and there will be peace.
I have a dream.

I have a dream, that all the adults and children in Africa
Will have fresh running water, instead of muddy, infected water.

I have a dream, that all the people in the world
Will be treated the same with no racism.
I have a dream today.

I have a dream, that elderly people
Will be treated with respect and dignity.

I have a dream, that everyone
Will have a home and family to go home to.
I have a dream today.

I have a dream, that every young child
Will have somebody to turn to.

I have a dream, that people
Will be loving and caring to animals.
I have a dream today.

I have a dream that every child
Deserves a good education.

*I have a dream today!*

**Jess Parker (12)**
Wellington School, Timperley


# My Mum

My mum is the best,
She gives me cuddles when I'm upset.
We have good times and bad,
But the best are when we have laughs.
I don't know what I would do if I didn't have you.
Mum, I love you.

**Holly Morrison (13)**
Wellington School, Timperley

# My Dream

I dreamed a dream
Of fairy tales to come true,
I dreamed a dream
With skies so blue.
I dreamed a dream
Of peace and love,
I dreamed a dream
Of God above.

I dreamed a dream
Of no violence or hate,
I dreamed a dream
It was so great,
I dreamed a dream
Of children playing,
I dreamed a dream
Where there was no slaying.
I dreamed a dream
Where no word went unheard,
I dreamed a dream
Of family and friends.

I dreamed a dream,
I dreaded to end.

**Tom Willington (12)**
Wellington School, Timperley


# To Travel The Sea!

If I were ever to travel the sea,
I'd make sure I had a friend with me.
If there were any fish,
I'd put them in a dish,
That is why I wish
To travel the sea.

**James Harris (12)**
Wellington School, Timperley

# Dreams

You never know what the future may hold,
When everything goes cold,
The heat from within will pull you through,
This is the heat of a dream.

There may be a cost,
And all may feel lost,
But there is always a light
At the end of the tunnel,
This is the light of a dream.

The world's full of pain,
But you can only gain
The knowledge and experience,
The knowledge and experience of a dream.

Life can be scary,
And things may get hairy,
But courage is all you need,
The courage of a dream.

Life is full of ups and downs,
Smiles and frowns,
But determination will triumph,
The determination of a dream.

**Darryl Andrew (12)**
Wellington School, Timperley

# I Have A Dream . . .

G oing around the world, yes, that is my dream.
L earning and looking at different people that don't all look the same.
O ff I go, off I go, I'm off to see the world.
B ig differences in the people, big differences in the places.
E nd of my trip, now my dream is done.
   The faces I've seen, the places I've been.
   Off I go, now I'm ready to plan my next big dream.

**Madison Constable (13)**
Wellington School, Timperley

# Imagine

I have no ideas tonight,
I have no inspiration,
I don't know what to write,
Imagine?
Imagine all the nations who have greater ideas than mine,
Imagine what they're imagining!
Imagine what the world could be like if I stood up
And my voice was heard?
I'm not sure,
But I think some people are doing this already.
I was hoping to come up with some of the most fantastic ideas,
I was hoping to be individual.
So what am I like?
I recently did a questionnaire, this is what I scored,
It said that I was:
Outgoing,
Enthusiastic,
Creative,
Successful
And adored.
Imagine if I could be like this for the rest of my life.
Imagine?

**Aimée Green (13)**
Wellington School, Timperley

# A Child's Life

Hit - scratch - punch - kick -
You've seen it all, you've felt the fist.
Now time is up, the clouds have cleared,
Those endless nights, always feared.

The terror found within your heart,
Replaced with loving and a happy start.
But can anyone actually heal your pain?
Across your heart, bears a stain.

The empty plates, the freezing rooms,
The messed up table, the house of doom,
The untouched present, the ruined clothes,
The empty tummy, the burnt out toes.

The glorious knock on the wooden front door,
A sign of people, it's them for sure?
They'd come to rescue, come to take,
Come to help, they knew he was fake.

In need of help, in need of love,
They took you and you felt like a dove,
Free in that world, away from that room,
Free from that house, that house of doom.

**Natasha Christopher (13)**
Wellington School, Timperley


# Love - I Had A Dream

1 picture of me
2 pictures of Mum
3 pictures of Dad
4 pictures of Gran
5 pictures of Nan
6 pictures of bro
7 pictures of sis
8 pictures of you because I *love* you.

**Sarah Moore (12)**
Wellington School, Timperley

# Searching Now

Searching now for inner space
Sure one day to find the place
What means of travel does one face?
This journey from the human race.

*Listen* sounds to tell they may
Or wait the stars to show way
Doth the soul to body say
*Suppress* all fears felt today?

If it's thought that moves the man
*Act* as if your thoughts still can
God designed this travel well
So we can move through Heav'n or Hell.

Take a trip, a different kind
*Open* channels in your mind
Inner space you soon will find
Are God and you intertwined?

The choice is yours, all's been planned
You can move through thought command
*Meditate* and *learn* first hand
Your mind controls this world so grand.

**Henry Doughty (12)**
Wellington School, Timperley


# Dream

I know how the dream goes,
It is the one I chose,
I think it will help you,
If it does it will help me too.
I have learned to love, to be nice,
To try and reach different heights,
You can't change me, no matter what you say,
This is the way I'm gonna stay.

**Beth Scorah (12)**
Wellington School, Timperley

# People . . .

People have rights,
People have power,
So we must fight for those rights,
Fight for that power
To gain what we want.

People have inspiration,
People have determination,
So we must keep that inspiration,
Keep that determination
To gain what we want.

People have heroes,
People have idols,
So we must remember them
To follow our dream.

People have friends,
People have family,
So we must respect those friends,
Love that family
To gain fulfilment,

And be happy.

**Helen Reading (13)**
Wellington School, Timperley

# A Friend Is . . .

Helpful in that special way,
Never tells you what to say,
My friends are special to me,
And always give me lots of glee,
They raise me up
So I can stand on mountains,
They raise me up
*To more than I can be!*

**Poppy Ward (13)**
Wellington School, Timperley

# I Have A Dream

I have a dream . . .
That all people in Africa can
Have food and water so they
Won't be hungry.

I have a dream . . .
That nobody will ever be
Poor and we are all
Healthy.

I have a dream . . .
That all orphan children get
A lovely happy family and
Life.

I have a dream . . .
That everyone deserves
And gets respect

I have a dream . . .
That the world will
Be a better place.

I have a dream today!

**Jade Diamond (12)**
Wellington School, Timperley


# I Have A Dream

Imagine a place where everyone can be equal,
Imagine a place where everybody can get along,
Imagine a place without war or fighting,
Just imagine what our world could be like.

Dream of a place without hunger or starvation,
Dream of a place without torture to others,
Dream of a place where things could be perfect,
Just make that dream come true.

**Lucy Haslam (13)**
Wellington School, Timperley

# I Have A Dream . . .

I have a dream that Nadia will stay by my side forever,
That she will never go away ever,
I have a dream that she will fight for me,
As many people as can be.
I have a dream she will love me forever,
As much as she will make me clever.
I have a dream that Nadia won't leave me in the dark
With all the monsters to steal my heart.
I have a dream that she will get rid of my greatest fear,
And then tell me to, 'Calm down dear.'
I have a dream that she will see,
That all my life is filled with glee.
I have a dream that we will stay in touch,
Even if you're learning Dutch.
I have a dream that she will never leave me alone,
And will never come to help me too slow.
I have a dream I will be with her,
Forever,
And ever,
And . . . ever.
My darling sister, Nadia.

**Saskia Palfreyman (12)**
Wellington School, Timperley

# Imagine Happiness

Imagine
Happy news making good news
And not good news making no news.
Imagine
Switching on the TV to find animal testing banned
Or that terrorists are no longer interested in aggression,
Just peace.
Imagine
The world becoming one big strong community.
Just imagine
If we were told that there was light at the end of the tunnel
Or sunshine after a storm.
No more racism, poverty, prejudice, terrorism or war.
Just imagine no more worries of global warming
Or people and animals dying.
Imagine a world full of happiness, peace,
Love and respect for others.
A world full of hopes and dreams.
Imagine being happy or feeling on top of the world
With nothing to bring you down.
Imagine!

**Emma Mash (12)**
Wellington School, Timperley

# Save

Save the world,
Save mankind
And save everyone who is kind.

Save the world,
Save the wild
And save my future child.

Save the world,
Save the sun
But send away the gun.

Save the world,
Save the light
And give animals a right.

Save the world,
Save the EU
And save me as well as you.

Save the world,
Save the dear
But send away the fear.

**Callum Smith (13)**
Wellington School, Timperley

# My Dream . . .

I have a dream,
I dream it all the time,
That out there, there is a mountain that I can climb,
I hope it's not that steep,
'Cause it will hurt my feet,

I have a dream,
I dream it all the time,
That one day there will be
A mountain for me to climb.

**Bethany Rooney (13)**
Wellington School, Timperley

# That Will Change

In the world I see
Lots of prejudice between him and me,
That will change.
Terrorism in Ireland,
Innocent families left crying for their loss,
That will change.
Helpless children without a mum,
Cancer taking its next victim,
That will change.
Racism in schools,
Bruises on children's arms,
That will change.
Abused women dreading going home,
An old man left all on his own,
That will change.
A man getting a fix for his son,
Not knowing if you will see the sun,
That will change,
I know it will change,
But not in my lifetime!

**Abigail Petitt (13)**
Wellington School, Timperley


# I Have A Dream

I have a dream that one day
The money made from taxes
Can be used to support our troops
Overseas and here in Britain,
And that while our military are fighting
For our protection
We will also be supporting our Emergency Services,
Who are battling for our protection in Britain,
And this is my dream.

**Frankie Atkins (13)**
Wellington School, Timperley

# I Have A Dream

People say dreams never come true . . .
But they are wrong, I know they do.
I dream of violence, I dream of hurt,
I dream of you, I dream of me.
I dream of how this was never meant to be.
I dream of my feelings, I dream of my thoughts,
I dream of my loved ones, I dream what I've said.
I dream of these thoughts exploding my head,
I dream of you yelling, I dream of you crying,
I dream of you hiding, I dream of you lying.
People say dreams never come true,
But they are wrong, I know they do.

I am a dreamer, but without dreams
What would this world be?
As empty as a heart that has no love,
As dark as night that has no stars.
I sleep so I must be a dreamer
And so I dream on,
As they come true, like I know they do . . .

**Olivia Plant (12)**
Wellington School, Timperley


# I Have A Dream

I have a dream
A national dream
That one day I will
Travel the world
Meet new people
See celebrities
And most of all
Live my life
In a beautiful
World!

**Victoria Bholé**
Wellington School, Timperley

# I Have A Dream

I have a dream
That one day
I will help the needy,
The poor, the hungry,
Put the rain in Africa
And wipe away their fears!

I have a dream,
For one day I will
See the world,
To India, Australia or even Peru,
See the sights
And be part of their life!

I have a dream
To complete school
GCSEs, A levels too,
To get a job,
Get some money
To help my family live their lives.

**Erin Sleater (12)**
Wellington School, Timperley


# I Have A Dream

I have a dream,
A wonderful dream,
To play basketball,
For every team.
To slam dunk that ball into the net
Would be an experience never to forget.

My life is basketball, that's what I do,
And when I grow up that's what I intend to do,
To bounce the ball round the other team,
Would let me accomplish my wonderful dream.

**Jacob Yates (12)**
Wellington School, Timperley

# Your Dream

What would you do
If you saw suffering around you?

What would you say
If you wanted to change the world today?

Would you go to the extreme
If no one was working as a team?

What risks would you take
If you didn't want to make a mistake?

Would you lend a hand
If it's come down to the final strand?

Can you achieve your dream
When it isn't as easy as it may seem?

But don't feel downhearted or glum
Just look at how far you've come!
Because in life you just need to believe,
Then you've won.

**Laura Knowles (12)**
Wellington School, Timperley


# I Have A Dream

I am inspired with a dream,
My dream drives me forward.
My inspiration comes from Ashley Jackson,
He gave me words of encouragement
And my head never dropped to the ground.
I now push and push to be the best,
Though I know I have a long way to go . . .
I wish to lead and captain the England hockey team,
Show them new heights and feats
And to take them to the top of the world.
That is my dream . . .

**Kieron George (12)**
Wellington School, Timperley

# Just Think

Just look around and what do you see?
Happiness, sadness or dignity?
Just look around and what do you see?
Peace, crime or liberty?
Just think to yourself and what do you feel?
Are you fighting for a better deal?
Just think to yourself and what do you feel?
Are you fighting for a healthy meal?
Just stand still and what do you hear?
Noise from the road that's near?
Just stand still and what do you hear?
Many things to scare and fear?
If you don't do something,
I sure will,
For all cruelty I shall kill,
Litter will go down,
Racism will be drowned,
And we shall all be happy!

**Kate Tomlinson (12)**
Wellington School, Timperley

# Mum

Mum
You always doubt yourself,
Oh yes you do,
You always think that you are poo,
But keep this poem in your mind,
And remember you're nothing but kind.
You do your best to keep us happy,
And loved us since we wore a nappy,
So keep a smile on your face,
And read this poem with love and grace,
Mum.

**Olivia Norris (12)**
Wellington School, Timperley

206

# A Hope, A Dream

Everyone needs inspiration,
Someone to look up to,
Everyone needs a view of the nation.

The people who inspire us,
Let them be at peace,
So that we listen to every word of their speech.

We'll never turn away,
We'll never disagree,
Let them be comforted by the tomorrow
You and me shall bring.

I can see beyond the fashion fads,
The fancy shoes, coats and bags,
I can see what should be done to see what I want to see.

There is never a better day than tomorrow,
I say that it can never bring sorrow,
Never worry, just trust the days to come.

**Georgina Howarth-Evans (13)**
Wellington School, Timperley


# You Choose

You choose to be together or to be one,
You choose to be sad or to have fun,
You choose to be good or to be bad,
You choose to be unique or follow a fad,
You choose.
We all have choices and mine is clear,
I choose to have a good career,
I know exactly what I want to be,
Being myself and being me.
I am an individual and I don't fit the mould,
My motto is to be big and bold!
You choose!

**Mollie Brooks (13)**
Wellington School, Timperley

# Who Inspires Me?

Who inspires me:

He has big bushy grey hair,
He hugs me when I'm scared,
I love him loads and loads
From his wrinkles to his toes.
He laughs and jokes with me,
But he watches really bad TV,
He likes to watch opera shows
And battling banjos.
I love him loads and loads
From his wrinkles to his toes.
He is one, oh, my best friend,
He can drive me around the bend,
I love him loads and loads
From his wrinkles to his toes.
Here he comes, he's looking bad,
He's my silly old grandad!

**Jake Crumbleholme (12)**
Wellington School, Timperley

# I Have A Dream

I have a dream to say goodbye,
I have a dream to see her smile just one more time.
I have a dream that we can laugh together again.
I have a dream that you are here with me
So we can fly and be free.
I have a dream to go to the park
With a friend that won't shut me in the dark.
I have a dream that you are here with me
Forever and ever till the time comes for me.
Amy, I never wanted you to leave,
I hated the day that you got carried away by the angels,
It broke my heart.

**Sarah Abbey (12)**
Wellington School, Timperley

# I Have A Dream

I have a dream,
A dream to swim,
To do something special
And maybe to win.

I have a dream,
A dream to swim across the seven seas,
To make my country proud
As I swim for GB.

I have a dream,
A dream for success,
To succeed in what I do
Without making a mess.

I have a dream,
A dream to tell,
A dream to make people happy,
So hopefully I'll do well.

**Hannah Barker (13)**
Wellington School, Timperley


# My Inspirations

There are inspirations out there,
No matter if they are near or far,
They touch our hearts and make us see,
They inspire you and they inspire me,
They give you hope,
Make you see the world colourful,
Like through a kaleidoscope.

Your inspiration makes you you,
They're always there, they're with you,
They will always help you pull through,
And that, you see, is why
My *family* and *friends* are the people who inspire me.

**Elfin Berry (13)**
Wellington School, Timperley

# I Have . . .

I have determination
To be an inspiration,
To inspire people
All across the nation.

My mum inspires me,
For everything she says,
Gives everyone she loves
Determination to succeed.

Everyone has a choice
To become who they want to be,
Don't listen to anyone else,
It's up to you.

Dream hard for a better world,
Dream, wish and hope,
Because whatever you will do
Will inspire others just to be like you!

**Alice Norris (13)**
Wellington School, Timperley


# My Poem

Do you have a hope?
Do you have a dream?
I want to go to university
I want to travel the world
I want to help people in Africa
But it's never going to happen
If I never work.
I need to try my hardest
To get to the very top,
But it's never going to happen
If I lack a lot.
I have a dream.

**Katie Ash (13)**
Wellington School, Timperley


210

# I Have A Dream

P  is for pandas being killed for
   their fur
O  is for orang-utans being kept in
   captivity
A  is for animals being
   killed
C  is for chinchillas being killed
   for their hair
H  is for homes/habitats being
   destroyed
I   is for injured
   animals
N  is for neglected
   animals
G  is for gorillas and their families
   destroyed.

**Ashley Sherlock (12)**
Wellington School, Timperley


# I Have A Dream . . .

I have a dream that one day tiny little rats and rabbits
Will be set free, and their torture will end,
So they can have the joy-filled life they deserve.

I have a dream that little mice
And little hamsters will not be tested on
With products that the world does not need.

I have a dream today
That monkeys and birds will not have just a few feet to walk,
But the whole world to roam.

I have a dream that helpless little cats and dogs
Aren't tied up to test our make-up and shampoo
That we do not need to use.

**Sam Johnston (13)**
Wellington School, Timperley

# I Have A Dream

I have a dream
To travel the world
To see different places
To see different people
To see every country
To see every flag
To see extraordinary landmarks
And see what's new
Seeing different animals
Going to Paris, London, Africa
Or Peru
Even places you never knew
Seeing different cultures
Seeing different religions
Eating different foods
That's my dream.

**Charlotte Callaghan (13)**
Wellington School, Timperley


# The Racer

My cousin Parker,
Using a marker,
To sign all his autographs.

He sped round a corner,
And took out a yawner,
Which ended his big race.

He went away,
During May,
In a car with flashing lights.

Now he stays at home
And he talks to his gnome,
And doesn't race anymore.

**Stephen Hoyland (12)**
Wellington School, Timperley

# I Have A Dream

Help
People in Africa
Help
People with Down's Syndrome
Help
People who can't walk
Help
People who are paralysed
Help
Children who are being abused
Help
Children who have to look after their families
Help
Children in need
Help
I have a dream to help the world!

**Charlotte Williams (12)**
Wellington School, Timperley

# My Dream

This little dream of mine,
It's something I'm determined to find,
A doctor,
A vet,
Then I'll be able to look after my pet.
Dentist,
Nurse,
I'll have some money in my purse.
Barnardos,
Children in need,
Families I will help to feed.
This little dream is mine,
It's something I'm determined to find!

**Cheyenne Sanders (13)**
Wellington School, Timperley

213

# I Have A Dream

I have a dream that guns and knife crime will stop
And everybody will be safe.
That people won't take things for granted
Even if they want to.
I have a dream that poverty will be a thing of the past
So that poor children around the world can last.
Black and white people are all the same
But it's not very nice when people shout racist names,
Mostly in vain.
I have a dream that wars in the world will end
And the peace and harmony will start to mend.
I have a dream that all people will be equal
And the world will be a better place.
I have a dream,
And I hope one day this dream will come true.

**Alex Ashton (13)**
Wellington School, Timperley


# I Have A Dream

I have a dream
To glide through the snow,
To jump over rocks,
To have a go.

I have a dream
To slide down mountains,
To never give up,
To see frozen fountains.

I have a dream
To jump over hills,
To see polar bears,
I feel the thrills.

*I have a dream.*

**Anne Mawson (13)**
Wellington School, Timperley

# My Dream

Dancing has always been a dream of mine,
I've been dancing since the age of nine,
When a beat comes on I feel a flow,
I can express my feelings and let them show,
It brings out a different person inside,
To be the best you've got, to set standards high,
To become big you have to believe,
Without any hope you'll never achieve.
So I'm going to carry on dancing and never give up,
I'm aiming high, in fact I'm aiming for the gold cup.
I have a dream and that's to be a dancer
And never am I getting the name of the local prankster,
Dancing has always been a dream of mine,
And tonight I've decided I'm going to let it shine.

**Izzie Walsh (12)**
Wellington School, Timperley

# Determination

Determination helps me succeed,
Makes me grit my teeth,
Making me feel I can do what I must
Against the odds,
Keeping me going,
Knowing not all is lost,
I can win!
Determination keeps me going,
Never letting me give in
Against the terrain,
Wind, snow, sun and rain,
Just the glimmer of hope gives me it,
I can win,
I am determined!

**Jack Owens (13)**
Wellington School, Timperley

# Imagine

Imagine travelling the world,
And seeing each flag,
Going to different countries,
And meeting someone called Mag.

Imagine travelling the world,
Seeing places you never knew,
Going round Paris, Greece, Africa,
Or even Peru.

Imagine travelling the world,
Looking at animals you've never seen,
Always going to remember it,
That's my dream!

**Megan Hart (13)**
Wellington School, Timperley

# Centre Stage

A single spotlight
In a world of injustice
The right to live comes
At a price.

What you make
Of what you've got
Is your choice to make
And yours alone.

Centre stage
A single spotlight
Your dreams are yours
*Your* choice is right.

**Alice Thomas (13)**
Wellington School, Timperley

# Imagine

Imagine
You had a dream.
Imagine
You stood out in a crowd.
Imagine
You made a difference.
Imagine
Your words changed the world.
Imagine
You helped thousands of people stand up.
Imagine
You were Martin Luther King.

**Michael Olin (13)**
Wellington School, Timperley

# Inspirations

I believe to be an inspiration
It takes hard work and determination,
It takes bravery and a fearless voice
Not relying on others to make your own choice.
It takes strength, goodness, helpfulness and caring,
Putting others before yourself, always sharing,
Treating every person with equal rights,
Petitioning for peace, finishing the fights.
So do what you can to get your say
Change someone's life, inspire someone today!

**Jenny Kirton (13)**
Wellington School, Timperley

# I Have A Dream

If I owned a horse
I would ride him every day.
If I owned a horse
I would groom him and groom him.
If I owned a horse
I would clean his tack until it was sparkly clean.
If I owned a horse
I'd love him forever and ever.
This is my dream,
And it will stay my dream.

**Hannah McKinnell (13)**
Wellington School, Timperley

# My Dream

I dreamed to jump out of a plane,
I dreamed to be of world fame.
I dreamed my voice was heard
Like a morning singing bird.
I dreamed people looked up to me,
Me and my whole family.
I dreamed that people didn't have to hide,
People wouldn't have had to lie.
I dreamed that all kids would be loved.

**Leon Grimes (12)**
Wellington School, Timperley

# War

*War*
Bodies lying dead on the floor
*War*
People dying here and there
*War*
What will happen I declare
*War*
Stop this madness
*War.*

**Jamie Hickman (13)**
Wellington School, Timperley

219

# Young Writers Information

We hope you have enjoyed reading this
book - and that you will continue to enjoy it
in the coming years.

If you like reading and writing poetry drop
us a line, or give us a call, and we'll send
you a free information pack.

Alternatively if you would like to order further
copies of this book or any of our other titles,
then please give us a call or log onto our
website at www.youngwriters.co.uk

Young Writers Information
Remus House
Coltsfoot Drive
Peterborough
PE2 9JX
(01733) 890066